DOES CHRISTIANITY TEACH MALE HEADSHIP?

The Equal-Regard Marriage and Its Critics

Edited by

David Blankenhorn
Don Browning
and
Mary Stewart Van Leeuwen

William B. Eerdmans Publishing Company
Grand Rapids, Michigan / Cambridge, U.K.

© 2004 Wm. B. Eerdmans Publishing Co.
All rights reserved

Wm. B. Eerdmans Publishing Co.
255 Jefferson Ave. S.E., Grand Rapids, Michigan 49503 /
P.O. Box 163, Cambridge CB3 9PU U.K.

Printed in the United States of America

09 08 07 06 05 04   7 6 5 4 3 2 1

Library of Congress Cataloging-in-Publication Data

Does Christianity teach male headship?: the equal-regard marriage and its critics/
   edited by David Blankenhorn, Don Browning, and Mary Stewart Van Leeuwen.
     p.   cm.
   Includes bibliographical references.
   ISBN 0-8028-2171-5 (pbk.: alk. paper)
   1. Marriage — Religious aspects — Christianity. 2. Equality — Religious
   aspects — Christianity. 3. Patriarchy — Religious aspects — Christianity.
   I. Blankenhorn, David. II. Browning, Don S. III. Van Leeuwen, Mary Stewart, 1943-
BT706.D63 2004
261.8′35872 — dc22

                         2004064209

www.eerdmans.com

DOES CHRISTIANITY TEACH MALE HEADSHIP?

RELIGION, MARRIAGE, AND FAMILY

Series Editors

Don S. Browning
David Clairmont

Contents

v

Contents

Series Foreword

The RELIGION, MARRIAGE, AND FAMILY series evolves out of a research project located at the University of Chicago and financed by a generous grant from the Division of Religion of the Lilly Endowment, Inc. The first phase of the project lasted from 1991 to 1997 and produced eleven books on religion and family. In late 1997, the Lilly Endowment gave the project an additional major grant that supports a second phase of research and publication. The books in the Eerdmans Religion, Marriage, and Family series come directly or indirectly from the initiatives of this second phase.

In some cases, the books will evolve directly out of the University of Chicago project. In other cases, they will be books written in response to that project or in some way stimulated by it. In all cases, they will be books probing the depth of resources in Judaism and Christianity for understanding, renewing, and in some respects redefining current expressions of marriage and family. The series will investigate issues of parenthood and children, work and family, responsible fatherhood, and equality in the family; the responsibility of the major professions in promoting and protecting sound marriages and families; the biblical, theological, philosophical, and legal grounds of Western family systems; selected classics of these traditions; and the respective roles of church, market, and state in supporting marriages, families, parents, and children.

The Religion, Marriage, and Family series intends to go beyond the sentimentality, political manipulation, and ungrounded assertions that characterize so much of the contemporary debate over marriage and family. It plans to develop an intelligent and accessible new literature for colleges and seminaries, churches and other religious institutions, questing individuals and families. Marriage and family issues are not just preoccupations of the United States; they have become worldwide concerns as modernization, globalization, changing values, emerging poverty, and changing gender roles disrupt traditional families and challenge the very idea of marriage throughout the world. It has been predicted that the emerging marriage and family crisis will be the central issue of the twenty-first century. The Religion, Marriage, and Family series hopes to contribute to more balanced and well-informed public debate on this issue, both in the United States and around the globe.

Many people believe that Christianity is the major cultural carrier of the subordination of women. The chapters in *Does Christianity Teach Male Headship?* debate whether this is true or not. The controversy often comes down to the relation of Christianity to its surrounding culture. Many of the authors hold that the idea that the male was the master of both wife and children came more from the surrounding Greco-Roman culture than it did from early Christianity itself. The early church, they argue, was born into a patriarchal honor-shame culture, was influenced by it, but was actually subtly undermining that very culture and its hierarchical social structures.

    Some authors argue that this was true in early Christianity, but it also was true at other times in the history of the church. Time and again it was difficult to tell whether Christianity looked profoundly patriarchal because that was its basic character or whether it appeared that way because surrounding secular, legal, and economic institutions had a vested interest in depicting Christian traditions that way.

    The open debate in this book includes Protestants and Roman Catholics, liberals and conservatives. Somewhat more liberal voices open the debate, but they don't go unchallenged. A real exchange of different views occurs. I think the book is perfect for classroom discussions in both the church and the academy. The tensions between the equal-regard marriage and the headship marriage are still with us and will be so for years to come.

DON S. BROWNING and DAVID CLAIRMONT
series editors

Acknowledgments

ALL OF US who participated in the discussions and wrote the papers that led to this volume are grateful to the Division of Religion of the Lilly Endowment, Inc., and to the John Templeton Foundation for their generous financial support of this project.

The Religion, Culture, and Family Project, based at the University of Chicago Divinity School and led by Don Browning, and also supported financially by the Lilly Endowment, played an important leadership — should I say headship? — role in making this book possible. David Brenner, as associate director of the Institute for American Values, played a key organizing and editorial role. Josephine Tramontano and Charity Navarrete, also on the Institute staff, ably performed the diverse administrative tasks connected to the project. Deb Strubel, a research associate at the Institute for American Values, provided important editorial assistance.

We are also deeply grateful to Iain T. Benson, Ellen Charry, Don Eberly, Elizabeth Fox-Genovese, Heather Higgins, Mardi Keyes, Thomas Kohler, Dana Mack, William Mattox, Gilbert Meilaender, Kenneth Schmitz, and J. Bradley Wigger for their participation in this project, and to Jon Pott, Jennifer Hoffman, Noelle Barkema, and others at Eerdmans Publishing for their commitment to this book and their skill in publishing it.

Introduction

David Blankenhorn

THE BEST ARGUMENT I ever heard for male headship in Christian families came from interviewing a group of women. They were members of the Apostolic Church of God, a thriving African-American Pentecostal church located on the South Side of Chicago. I was doing research on fatherhood and wanted their views.

I asked them, "Is the father the head of the family?" Yes, they all said, that's what the Bible teaches. "Well," I continued, "what does it mean to be the head of the family?" On this point, the women were equally united and emphatic. It means working hard to support the family financially. It means leading the family in prayer at meal times. And it means taking the family to church on Sundays.

I wanted to press them further, perhaps shake their confidence. I asked, "But aren't mothers and wives equally capable of leadership? For example, when I visited the children's Sunday school classes this morning, I noticed that all of the teachers were men. Aren't you women just as qualified to teach those classes?"

Several of the women smiled. Others looked at me intently and patiently. Yes, they all told me, we could teach those classes. And for many years, before the pastor decided some time ago that all Sunday school classes would be taught by men, we *did* teach them. But we *want* our men to teach those classes, for the same reason that they must serve as the heads of our families. And the reason is that we know the alternative. We see it all around us, every day. That alternative is drugs, prison, and early death. That's the choice that our men must make, and we praise God for those who make the right choice.

It's not ultimately a question of who has the capacity or the right, these women seemed to be telling me. It's not even a question of natural ability, or of who can do the best job. Indeed, to me these women seemed completely confident of their ability and, in a deep sense, their authority in almost all matters related to their children. Rather, it seemed to be a question of finding a clear job within the family (and also in the church) that the man can perform well — a kind of status or office, some of it ceremonial and symbolic, that he can understand, aspire to, and fulfill successfully, for his own sake and for the good of his family and community, in keeping with traditional Christian teaching.

For these men on the more dangerous side of the tracks in South Side Chicago, what is the alternative? If they are not the heads of their families, what part are they? The appendix? An extra pair of hands? Someone who tries, and as often as not fails, to do exactly what the mother is doing? Good luck! Not much chance for high success there. Not much chance for honor, nor much realistic recognition of the role of testosterone in male affairs — that is, the man's need to compete with other men and to feel that he is doing something important in life that requires strength, endurance, and self-sacrifice.

I often hear a fainter, more relaxed version of this argument from more secular, affluent women. For example, I once asked a group of white, middle-class, married mothers in Cleveland, Ohio, "Is the father the head of the family?" Well, something along those lines, seemed to be the rough consensus, although none of these women appeared to be quaking in their high heels, overcome with deference. A number of them found the question amusing. One woman said, "Yeah, I run the train, but I let him blow the whistle."

We love them and need them, these women seemed to be saying — in fact, most married mothers today report that they get a much better deal from their husbands than their mothers got from their fathers — but it takes effort to educate them and they do need clear job descriptions and no small amount of reminding. An office, a status. Look at me: I wear a handsome cap, look out the window, and blow the whistle.

How important is this issue of trying to craft an esteemed role for the male within the family? Surely the answer depends in large measure on the degree to which we as a society are worried about today's trend of widespread fatherlessness.[1] For those who are not overly alarmed by

1. Commission on Children at Risk, *Hardwired to Connect: The New Scientific Case*

the fact that millions of fathers today are separated from the lives of their children and estranged from the mothers of their children — or perhaps more precisely, for those whose desire to reverse this societal trend is at least matched by their desire to institutionalize a certain model of equalitarian, largely androgynous gender roles — bothering at all over this thorny question of headship, or the male office in the family, is probably too high a price to pay. Aren't we beyond all that? But for those who feel otherwise — as the women from the Apostolic Church of God in Chicago certainly do — are there many questions facing our society today that could be more important?

The best argument I ever heard *against* male headship in Christian families is the very traditional Christian teaching that man is sinful. Man — and here I mean both "person" as well as, especially, "the male" — is prone to pridefulness and to what Augustine calls the lust for domination *(libido dominandi).* We want to control, we often seek to coerce, in our weakness we want to inflate ourselves by compelling others toward obedience. This is part of the human condition. It is also, across time and cultures, a very visible component of the male sexual repertoire.[2]

There is more. Our Christian tradition also teaches us that man, when he philosophizes, has a marked tendency to indulge his pride and to seek to rationalize his lust for domination — to fall prey when explaining himself to what some Christian thinkers have called the noetic effects of sin.[3] A small example to illustrate: When a heavy drinker with a fine wine cellar and a Ph.D. is constantly citing research suggesting that drinking red wine is good for one's health, we are probably witnessing, at least in part, the noetic or intellectual effects of sin.

As far as historians can determine, marriage as a social institution

---

for Authoritative Communities (New York: Institute for American Values, 2003), pp. 40-41. See also Wade F. Horn, David Blankenhorn, and Mitchell B. Pearlstein, eds., *The Fatherhood Movement* (Lanham, Md.: Lexington Books, 1999); and Obie Clayton, Ronald B. Mincy, and David Blankenhorn, eds., *Black Fathers in Contemporary American Society* (New York: Russell Sage Foundation, 2003).

2. See Margo Wilson and Margo Daly, "An Evolutionary Psychological Perspective on Male Sexual Proprietariness and Violence Against Wives," in R. B. Rubacker and N. A. Weiner, eds., *Interpersonal Violent Behaviors* (New York: Springer Publishing, 1995).

3. See Jean Bethke Elshtain, *Augustine and the Limits of Politics* (Notre Dame: University of Notre Dame Press, 1995), pp. xii, 105-12.

among human beings first came into being in the Nile and Tigris-Euphrates river valleys about 5,000 years ago. There, for the first time, humans began saying for the record what marriage is — formulating laws to define and govern the new institution, writing instruction manuals for the young on how to court and marry, and creating lasting art showing married couples.[4]

To my eye, much of this early history of marriage is beautiful and instructive. Many of the early law codes, for example, are painstakingly detailed, covering all of the issues related to the marriage contract and bond that seem familiar to us today: broken engagements, pregnancies prior to marriage, spousal cruelty, grounds for divorce, penalties for spousal desertion, grounds for remarriage, support for widows, and so on.[5] These codes frequently specify the protections and rights due to wives. Much of the art is moving and intimate: We recognize these early married couples in Egypt and Mesopotamia as not too different from ourselves.

At the same time, we must also confront carefully the fact that the invention of marriage coincides with, and reflects, the domestic institutionalization of what we now call patriarchy. Notwithstanding the noteworthy protections given to wives, the question of headship in these societies — by which I mean who is the boss — is not hard to figure out. The men who formed these laws had a clear philosophy. A Middle Assyrian law concerning divorce dating from about 1500 BCE says: "If a [man of standing] wishes to divorce his wife, if it is his will, he may give her something; if it is not his will, he need not give her anything; she shall go out empty."[6]

This idea of headship, so closely connected to the ideals of patriarchy (literally, "father-beginning"), was later, of course, appropriated and developed further by other civilizations, including perhaps most notably the three Abrahamic religions of Judaism, Christianity, and Islam, each of which also emerged from that remarkable corner of the world. The dimensions and consequences of this amazing development

---

4. John W. Miller, "The Troubled Dawn of Fatherhood," Working Paper 74 (New York: Institute for American Values, 2000). I am indebted to Professor Miller for introducing me to this history.

5. James B. Pritchard, ed., *Ancient Near Eastern Texts* (Princeton: Princeton University Press, 1950), pp. 159-98.

6. Middle Assyrian Laws, No. 37, in Pritchard, *Ancient Near Eastern Texts*, p. 183.

are still very much with us today, and form the context for the debates in this book regarding the male's family role in Christianity.

Headship concerns marriage, of course, but also more than marriage. Frequently in Christian and Western history, the idea of headship has contained vital meanings for politics as well as for domestic life. For example, Britain's Sir Robert Filmer, in his seventeenth-century book *Patriarcha*, famously defends monarchical government by linking it to male headship in the family — a state of affairs which Filmer in turn traces to, and justifies with, God's words to Eve ("he shall rule over thee") as recorded in the book of Genesis.[7] For Filmer, and for others, the divine and absolute right of the king to rule the nation flowed directly from the divine and absolute right of the father to rule the family.

This philosophical and political legacy of headship, and more broadly patriarchy, makes many modern people wary and uncomfortable. There are very few Filmerites today. Many theologians who examine the issue discern the noetic effects of sin, at least regarding some of the more full-throated rationales for patriarchy. Even among those scholars who urge us to recognize the necessity and appreciate the importance of this basic way of ordering domestic life, there is also usually a clear recognition of the excesses and abuses, particularly regarding the rights and treatment of women, that have all too frequently been a part of this regime.

Where does that leave us? It leaves us with hard dilemmas. Can modern people of faith find sustainable ways to build lasting marriages and bind the male to the mother-child unit? Or must we learn to accept the steady untying of the marriage knot? Is there a specifically *male* family role that is both desirable and realistic? Or is any socially defined male role (other than the embrace of androgyny) unacceptable, taking us too close to authoritarianism and injustice?

The invention of marriage surely stands as one of the human species' greatest and most important cultural achievements. Perhaps most

---

7. We learn in Genesis 3:15-16 that, after the fall, God places "enmity" between the man and woman and tells Eve that her husband "shall rule over thee." Taking a cue from a number of analysts, I personally have come to understand these verses in much the same way that I understand God's statement in Deuteronomy 5:9 that children in future generations will be punished for "the sins of the fathers" — less as a divine prescription, something that God wants or intends for us, than as a description of what happens to us as a result of our sinfulness.

importantly, by bringing together the male and female of the species into enduring sexual union, it has decisively improved the human infant's chance to survive and flourish, in large measure by instituting for the child the protection and nurture of a father. Marriage's benefits extend not only to children, and to society as a whole, but also to individual husbands and wives. Loving, permanent marriage is one of the finest things that we humans are made for.

Today, of course, that institution has weakened considerably. Some scholars even suggest that we may be heading in the direction of a post-nuclear, or post-marriage, family system.[8] Perhaps that is true. But no one really knows, since the outcome will depend on the choices we make. The available data, as well as (I think) basic Christian epistemology, tell us that the future of marriage is less an externally defined or preordained process than an event in freedom.

There is some encouraging demographic news. Since about 1995, at least in the United States, many of the marriage-weakening trends of the past several generations have either slowed down considerably or stopped altogether.[9] Some negative trends may actually be reversing. For example, the proportion of African-American children living in two-parent, married-couple homes rose more than four percent from 1995 to 2000.[10] More broadly, growing numbers of people — including, in the U.S., the leaders of a grass-roots marriage renewal movement[11] — are actively searching for ways to reinvigorate marriage as a social institution.

For those people, anchored in hope and buoyed by some recent good news, these ancient questions of the male-female relationship within marriage have become obviously and centrally important, as current as this morning's newspaper headline and full of practical implications for their work. Here, especially from the perspective of today's marriage renewal movement, are several of these questions:

8. David Popenoe, *Disturbing the Nest: Family Change and Decline in Modern Societies* (New York: Aldine de Gruyter, 1988), p. 295.

9. David Blankenhorn, "The Marriage Problem," *American Experiment Quarterly* (Minneapolis: Center of the American Experiment, Spring 2003): 61-71.

10. Allen Dupree and Wendell Primus, *Declining Share of Children Lived with Single Mothers in the Late 1990s* (Washington, D.C.: Center on Budget and Policy Priorities, June 15, 2001).

11. See *The Marriage Movement: A Statement of Principles* (New York: Institute for American Values, 2000).

1. What is the best and truest way of understanding gender relations in the Christian family?
2. Is the husband the head of the family? Or should the headship model give way, either largely or entirely, to what a number of the contributors to this volume call the "equal regard" model?
3. What male family role is most possible and desirable in light of the increasingly recognized societal need to reconnect fathers to families?
4. Which if any models of male headship are consistent with the requirements of justice and with the equal dignity of all persons?

Wrestling with these and similar questions is the essence of this volume. The authors agree on the importance of the questions, but not at all on the answers. The contributors to Part I of the book make the case for equal-regard marriage. The contributors to Part II both critique that case and offer some of their own preferred alternatives, including the traditional headship model and what a number of thinkers, particularly those following the writings on this issue by Pope John Paul II, call the model of mutual submission. All of these essays, I believe, are intellectually and morally serious.

As a coeditor of the book, I am particularly pleased that the contributors not only offer strong and contrasting views but also specifically debate one another and substantively engage one another's essays, often on a point-by-point basis. The result is a book that reads less like a series of discrete presentations, each standing basically alone, than like a very high-level discussion, full of lively give-and-take. Enjoy.

PART I **EQUAL REGARD**

CHAPTER 1

The Problem of Men

Don Browning

WHAT VALIDITY is there to the popular belief that Christianity teaches male headship and for this reason is a chief carrier of patriarchy and female oppression? Honesty requires us to acknowledge that the entire ancient world was in some sense patriarchal and that all of its religions, including primitive Christianity, were implicated in the elevation of males over females. But this confession opens a deeper question: in what direction was the Jesus movement we now call Christianity actually moving on family and gender issues? Was early Christianity in tension with, and subtly undermining, what many scholars now call the "honor-shame codes" of the Greco-Roman world and their embeddedness in patriarchy?

There are good reasons to believe that the earliest forms of Christianity were in conflict on gender issues with their surrounding cultures. When our information is placed in context, it becomes clear that early Christian communities, along with aspects of Stoicism, functioned to mitigate male power and elevate women. Furthermore, their theological direction was to bring the principle of neighbor love or "equal regard" into the center of family life and the husband-wife relation. Love as equal in marriage means that both husband and wife should treat each other as ends — as persons — and never as means to other ends, i.e., as objects of manipulation. Within this mutual respect, they also should work equally for each other's good. This means they should strive to provide in principle equal access to the privileges and responsibilities of both the public sphere of politics and employment and the domestic sphere of child care and household duties. Self-sacrificial love, in this view, has a place but is not an end in itself;

it is, instead, that extra effort needed to restore broken relationships to mutuality and equal regard once again.

This was the argument of *From Culture Wars to Common Ground: Religion and the American Family Debate,* the summary book of the Religion, Culture, and Family Project.[1] In the early days of this project, biblical scholar David Balch (co-author with Carolyn Osiek of *Families in the New Testament World*) often said at our seminars, "The early Christian family was the Greco-Roman family with a twist."[2] With this formula, he reminded us that in urban centers throughout the Middle East the relation of the family to society (the polis) was defined predominantly by Hellenistic philosophical traditions. Specifically, it was shaped by Aristotle's threefold household theory about the tyrannical rule of master over slave, the aristocratic rule of husband over wife, and the monarchical rule of father over children. Aristotle's views had been spread by his student Alexander the Great throughout the Mediterranean world and later mingled with the Roman Empire, creating what we now call Roman Hellenism.

Pronouncements of the Southern Baptist church on the biblical mandate for wives to submit to husbands failed to identify this source of the male-headship tradition. It is, however, commonly known among New Testament scholars, including those in Southern Baptist institutions. This threefold theory can be found in both Aristotle's *Nicomachean Ethics* and his *Politics*.[3] Because it was part of the culture of the day, this Aristotelian family theory worked its way into the texts of early Christianity and can be found in Ephesians 5:21-33, Colossians 3:18-25, and 1 Peter 3:1-7. To give an example, note the threefold structure of the Colossians passage: "Wives, be subject to your husbands. . . . Children, obey your parents in everything. . . . Slaves, obey . . . your earthly masters."

---

1. Don Browning, Bonnie Miller-McLemore, Pamela Couture, K. Brynolf Lyon, and Robert Franklin, *From Culture Wars to Common Ground: Religion and the American Family Debate,* 2nd ed. (Louisville: Westminster/John Knox, 2000). This was the summary book of the eleven-volume Religion, Culture, and Family Project, located at the University of Chicago, and funded by the Division of Religion of the Lilly Endowment, Inc.

2. For the development of this point of view, see Carolyn Osiek and David Balch, *Families in the New Testament World: Households and House Churches* (Louisville: Westminster/John Knox, 1997).

3. Aristotle, *Politics* 1.12, and *Nicomachean Ethics,* in *The Basic Works of Aristotle,* ed. Richard McKeon (New York: Random House, 1941).

To catch the parallel with Aristotle, it helps to hear the philosopher's own words. In *Politics*, he wrote, "Of household management . . . there are three parts — one is the rule of a master over slaves, another of a father, and the third of a husband." In the *Nicomachean Ethics*, he gets more specific:

> For the association of a father with his sons bears the form of monarchy, since the father cares for his children. . . . Tyrannical too is the rule of master over slaves; for it is the advantage of the master that is brought about in it. . . . The association of man and wife seems to be aristocratic; for the man rules in accordance with his worth.[4]

Christianity and the Honor-Shame Culture

To further understand early Christian families as a "twist" on Greco-Roman patterns, Professor Osiek directed us to the anthropological and historical work on the honor-shame codes governing male-female behavior in ancient Mediterranean areas. These codes had much in common with Aristotle's philosophical formulations of worth (or honor) and their implications for family hierarchies. The codes reflect what many scholars call an "agonistic" culture, a culture organized around conflicts between men over issues of honor. In such cultures honor was associated with male dominance and agency while shame was associated with male weakness and passivity.[5] A sign of male weakness and shame was permitting the violation of the women of a man's household — wife, sister, or mother — without proper defense or retaliation. To keep such encroachments from happening, males enforced the systematic restriction of women to the domestic sphere.[6] If such an offense did occur, any self-respecting male was to challenge and subdue the violator with physical force. At the same time, free men were entitled to a great deal of public, political, and sexual freedom. They also

4. Aristotle, *Nicomachean Ethics* 8.10.

5. Halvor Moxnes, "Honor and Shame," *Biblical Theology Bulletin* (Winter 1993): 167-76.

6. David Cohen, *Law, Sexuality, and Society* (Cambridge: Cambridge University Press, 1991).

could gain honor if they could get away with shaming other men by seducing or offending the women in their households.

Although primitive Christianity never completely escaped the honor-shame codes of Roman Hellenism, it did fracture or partially undermine them.[7] The early church required Christian men to restrict their sexual activity to their wives. The church also rejected the agonistic challenge-riposte pattern of the Greco-Roman male-honor code. The ancient custom of infanticide, largely practiced when men for various reasons rejected their unwanted infants, was condemned by early Christian communities. Christian men were exhorted to imitate in their family relations Christ's sacrificial love for the church (Eph. 5:25). Women helped administer the love feast in the early Christian house churches and exercised leadership in evangelism.[8]

The new patterns between males and females occurring in the ecclesia spilled over into the everyday domestic life of early Christians. Husbands and wives related in more egalitarian ways at home, following patterns first established at their house churches. This happened to such an extent that early Christian families were seen by their pagan neighbors as threatening the official relation of family to polis in ancient cities, provoking authorities to persecute them for offenses to the established order. This in turn precipitated a retrenchment on gender equality in the post-Pauline church, as we see in 1 Peter.[9]

Ephesians versus Aristotle

Those who believe that early Christianity was an intentional teacher of male headship must confront this question: what direction was early Christianity going on this issue? Additional evidence is found that it experimented with new ideas on gender relations if we compare Ephesians 5:21-33 to Aristotle's theory of male responsibility in *Politics* and

7. Bruce Malina, *The New Testament World: Insights from Cultural Anthropology* (Louisville: Westminster/John Knox, 1993).

8. Stephen Barton, "Paul's Sense of Place: An Anthropological Approach to Community Formation in Corinth," *New Testament Studies* 32 (1986): 74.

9. For an interpretation of 1 Peter that shows this letter as an apology to pagan authorities for the alleged new freedoms in Christian families, see David Balch, *Let Wives Be Submissive: The Domestic Code in 1 Peter* (Atlanta: Scholars Press, 1981).

Nicomachean Ethics. First, Ephesians begins with a radical injunction toward mutuality of husband and wife: "Be subject to one another out of reverence to Christ" (5:21). This precedes and frames the soon-to-follow words asking wives to be "subject" to their husbands (5:22). Aristotle, on the other hand, spoke of a proportional equity between husband and wife ("the man rules in accordance with his worth") and a constitutional aristocracy of the husband over the wife based on this superior worth. There is nothing approaching the idea of mutual subjection between husband and wife to be found in Aristotle's thought.

Second, Ephesians based this mutual subjection on reverence for Christ. Aristotle, on the other hand, grounded proportional equity in the alleged higher deliberative powers of males. Aristotle writes, "For although there may be exceptions to the order of nature, the male is by nature fitter for command than the female."[10]

Third, Ephesians tells husbands to love their wives as Christ loves the church, thereby developing a theory of male servanthood. Aristotle, on the other hand, writes that the higher honor should go to the better: "The friendship of man and wife, again, is the same that is found in an aristocracy; for it is in accordance with virtue — the better gets more of what is good."[11]

Finally, Ephesians tells us that husbands should love "their wives as they do their own bodies. . . . For no one ever hates his own body, but he nourishes and tenderly cares for it, just as Christ does for the church, because we are members of his body" (5:28-30). In these words we hear the love commandment — "You shall love your neighbor as yourself" (Matt. 22:39) — brought directly into the inner precincts of marital relations. Nothing similar to this can be found in Aristotle or, for the most part, in other pagan philosophical writings on marriage and family.

Christian Neighbor Love and the "Male Problematic"

These striking contrasts between Aristotle and Ephesians do not completely deliver early Christianity from patriarchy, but they suggest that its trajectory is away from it. It is generally thought that the principle

10. Aristotle, *Politics* 1.12.
11. Aristotle, *Nicomachean Ethics* 8.11.

of neighbor love is the interpretive center of Christian ethics. We learn this in Jesus' response to the lawyer who asked, "Teacher, which commandment in the law is the greatest?" In answering, Jesus lists first the command to love God with all our heart, soul, and mind, and second the command, "You shall love your neighbor as yourself." It follows from this, I argue, that the present task of Christian theology is to complete the early church's critique of male headship with its associated honor-shame code and finish the task of implementing its direction toward a marriage ethic of equal regard.

But the idea of neighbor love — and the concept of equal regard between husband and wife that it implies — does not give a complete ethic for families. More is needed. In *From Culture Wars to Common Ground,* we took the concept of male servanthood very seriously. Fathers and husbands, in being servants to their families, are not only contradicting ancient honor-shame patterns, they are imitating — indeed recapitulating — the nature of God as revealed in the love of Christ. This is a very heady idea, but one worth pondering. It may reveal something profound about the nature of humans, the nature of God, and the uniqueness of Christian family theory.

Insight into the meaning of early Christianity's redefinition of male responsibility can be discovered in some startling formulations of Christian family theory made by Thomas Aquinas. In his "Supplement" to the *Summa Theologica* and in *Summa contra Gentiles,* Aquinas made remarkable observations, quite consistent with some modern social science views, about the natural needs that lead to the formation of human families.[12] These observations do not constitute a Christian theory of marriage and family as such, but they do provide insights into the natural conditions of family formation that should be kept in mind when building a Christian view. Aquinas's observations deepen understanding of why human males became involved in families, generally with considerable ambivalence. They also help us to see how Christianity used concepts and symbols that both appealed to these natural tendencies and transformed them, thereby helping to stabilize Christian male commitment to children and wives.

For instance, Aquinas was aware, as is contemporary evolutionary

12. See Thomas Aquinas, *Summa Theologica,* "Supplement" (New York: Benziger Brothers, 1948), and *Summa contra Gentiles* (London: Oates and Washbourne, 1928), 3.ii.

theory,[13] that human males are unique among animals in learning to care for their progeny and becoming attached to their consorts. Other male primates, for the most part, do not help care for their infants after fathering them. Aquinas advanced several reasons why human males became involved in families over the course of history. He listed (1) the long period of human infant dependency that leads the female to demand help from her sexual partner in raising their offspring, (2) the recognition by a human male that a particular child is most likely his and therefore a part of his very biological existence, (3) sexual exchange that integrates the male into a more stable relation with his female partner (following Paul, he called it paying the "marital debt"), and (4) mutual assistance between male and female that further consolidates their relationship. These are natural reasons Aquinas gives for how human males are pulled into long-term relationships with offspring and consorts.

It is widely known that Thomas Aquinas believed marriage to be an unbreakable sacrament, but a very important part of that theory is almost always overlooked. The logic of his argument for the permanence of marriage reveals that he wanted a ground for stabilizing fragile male commitment to families. He was aware that a human female knows with certainty that the infant she births is hers; for instance, she experiences the burdens of pregnancy and the trials of delivery. Males have much more tentative and difficult-to-discern relations to the infants they father. Behind Aquinas's theory of sacramental permanence of the marital bond was his insight into human male ambivalence about fatherhood — an ambivalence that I sometimes call the "male problematic."

Aquinas was similar to contemporary evolutionary biologists in his awareness that human males are almost unique among mammals in their capacity to bond with their children and mates. I agree with John Miller in his *Biblical Faith and Fathering* that stabilizing male responsibility and giving it sacred meaning was one of the great accomplishments of both Judaism and Christianity.[14] Both faiths depicted

13. See, for instance, the work of Don Symons, *The Evolution of Sexuality* (Oxford: Oxford University Press, 1979); Pierre Van den Berghe, *Human Family Systems* (New York: Elsevier, 1979); and Martin Daly and Margo Wilson, *Sex, Evolution, and Behavior* (Belmont: Wadsworth, 1978).

14. John Miller, *Biblical Faith and Fathering* (New York: Paulist, 1989).

God as a caring father whom human males were commanded to imitate. Whether one takes Aquinas's sacramentalism literally or symbolically, we find in his thought additional helpful insight into this transformation of men into fathers.

Modern evolutionary biology and psychology recognize variations of the same four natural factors leading to family formation that Aquinas discussed. Aquinas's thought is in many ways better, however — fuller and less reductionistic. His worldview adds much that evolutionary psychologists generally overlook. They do contribute, nevertheless, an important additional theory — the theory of "kin altruism." (Aquinas took over something like this theory from Aristotle but never explicitly stated it.) Kin altruism is the idea that all creatures, including humans, are more likely to invest in and sacrifice for those who share their own genes than they are for nonkin. Aquinas had no theory of genes, but both he and evolutionary biology believe that the reality of kin preference is a major, although not the only, factor behind paternal recognition and investment.

Certainly Christian love and self-sacrifice add more to the motivation of Christian fathers, but these virtues build on and guide natural kin altruism. Kin altruism is a finite and partial value not to be ignored, suppressed, or disregarded. It is to be encouraged, developed, extended, and transformed. When it becomes idolatrous, it must also be constrained. The highest commitment of Christians should be to the Kingdom of God, not their own kin; but within that framework, as Aquinas well knew, the energies of kin altruism have their rightful place.

Both Aquinas and evolutionary theory, however, believe that more is required to truly stabilize male investment. Aquinas went so far as to interpret the Ephesians analogy between Christ's sacrificial love for the church and a husband's love for his family as having the clear intent of stabilizing male hesitancy to bond. Ephesians and Aquinas had different analyses of this problematic, but both see Christian symbols as addressing and overcoming it.

Christianity and the World Fatherhood Problem

Family changes are occurring throughout the world. We generally overlook, however, the fact that the central feature of these changes is that more and more children are raised without the guidance of their fathers. One-third of all children in the United States are presently living apart from their biological fathers; nearly one-half live apart from their fathers for a period of three years before the age of eighteen. Princeton sociologist Sara McLanahan has demonstrated on the basis of the analysis of large sets of demographic data that children raised apart from their two biological parents are two to three times more likely to do poorly in school, have difficulty getting jobs, and have children out of wedlock.[15] The Western religious tradition, evolutionary theory, and empirical evidence all suggest that fathers are important. From a Christian perspective, having a committed father is not a guarantee of salvation; but it does on average contribute to the health and strength of children and is an important order of society to be preserved.

In *From Culture Wars to Common Ground,* we acknowledged that many conservative religious forces of our society — Protestant evangelicalism, the African-American church, and the Roman Catholic Church — are more aware of the male problematic than liberal religious movements. To this extent, Southern Baptists and the Promise Keepers, with their emphasis on male responsibility, have their finger on something important. But these groups are wrong in believing that male responsibility must necessarily be coupled with models of male headship. They seem to suggest that a little soft patriarchy is the price to be paid for male responsibility.

I agree that there is something important in the idea of male servanthood, but not necessarily in male servant headship. I recommend following Paul's belief that servanthood should apply to both wives and husbands: "For the unbelieving husband is made holy through his wife, and the unbelieving wife is made holy through her husband" (1 Cor. 7:14). Although my colleagues and I argue in *From Culture Wars to Common Ground* that the equal regard implicit in neighbor love is the heart of the Christian theory of marital obligation, we follow Aquinas and his contemporary disciples in locating self-sacrifice (the cross) as a moment of loving steadfastness, renewal, and grace within love as mutuality.

The self-sacrifice of the cross, in this view, is not an end in itself, but tries to restore love as equal regard when it is in crisis and out of

---

15. Sara McLanahan and Gary Sandefur, *Growing Up with a Single Parent* (Cambridge: Harvard University Press, 1994).

balance.[16] In this respect both husband and wife are called to bear the cross in relation to each other and to their children, albeit in the service of love as equal regard.

16. Some neo-Thomistic statements of the role of self-sacrifice in service of marital love as mutuality and equal regard can be found in the following: Louis Janssens, "Norms and Priorities of a Love Ethics," *Louvain Studies* (1977): 207-37; Barbara Andolsen, "Agape in Feminist Ethics," *Journal of Religious Ethics* 9 (Spring 1981): 69-81; Christine Gudorf, "Parenting, Mutual Love, and Sacrifice," in *Woman's Consciousness, Woman's Conscience: A Reader in Feminist Ethics*, ed. Barbara Andolsen et al. (New York: Harper and Row, 1985).

CHAPTER 2

Is Equal Regard in the Bible?

Mary Stewart Van Leeuwen

IN THE LATE 1980s two evangelical organizations were formed with quite different agendas captured in quite different names: "The Council on Biblical Manhood and Womanhood" and "Christians for Biblical Equality." Each issued a statement about gender relations that it claimed was based on a high view and a close reading of the Bible, but the two groups came to very different conclusions. The Council on Biblical Manhood and Womanhood deplored "the increasing promotion given to feminist egalitarianism" and stated that "Adam's headship in marriage was established by God before the Fall, and was not a result of sin." Although affirming that "both Adam and Eve were created in God's image, equal before God as persons," and that "in the church, redemption in Christ gives men and women an equal share in the blessings of salvation," the Council's founders went on to say that "nevertheless, some governing or teaching roles within the church are restricted to men."[1]

The statement of Christians for Biblical Equality took quite a different approach. In its reading of the Bible, men and women were created for full and equal partnership. Further, Adam's rule over Eve occurred only as a result of the fall, and "through faith in Jesus Christ we all become children of God . . . heirs to the blessings of salvation without reference to racial, social or gender distinctives." Consequently, in

---

1. Council on Biblical Manhood and Womanhood, "The Danvers Statement," *Christianity Today* (Jan. 13, 1989): 40-44; John Piper and Wayne A. Grudem, eds., *Recovering Biblical Manhood and Womanhood: A Response to Evangelical Feminism* (Wheaton, Ill.: Crossway, 1991).

marriage "neither spouse is to seek to dominate the other, but each is to act as servant of the other . . . [sharing] responsibilities of leadership on the basis of gifts, expertise and availability." And in the church, "spiritual gifts of women and men are to be recognized, developed and used . . . at all levels of involvement."[2]

Here we have two very different stances on relations between men and women in church and home by two groups both of whom believe that the Bible is the inspired Word of God. Nor are these two stances the only ones circulating, for even more recently Pope John Paul II has gone on record as endorsing equality between husband and wife in marriage, while continuing to deny that women can serve as priests in the church. Conversely, Bill McCartney, the founder and CEO of the men's evangelical group known as Promise Keepers, has no trouble accepting women as ordained pastors but is adamant that the Bible calls for male headship in families. What is the average church member to do with these mixed messages? And just how important is the question of male headship, anyway?

To respond to the second of these questions first, we can point out that neither evangelical group treats male headship as a confessional issue — that is, one which is used as a litmus test for deciding who is a Christian and who is not. Even the Council on Biblical Manhood and Womanhood called its statement a list of "affirmations" — not "doctrines" or "confessions" — and its writers were careful to recognize "the genuine evangelical standing of many who do not agree with all of our convictions."[3] On the other side of the debate, a biblical scholar belonging to Christians for Biblical Equality once suggested that belief in male headship has been the source of so much abuse toward women that, like the earlier theological defense of apartheid in South Africa, it should be treated as not just a moral failure but an actual heresy. But even this critic finally adopted milder language, calling belief in male headship "a misguided form of the gospel as presented in the New Testament."[4] In general, Christians for Biblical Equality has

---

2. Christians for Biblical Equality, "Men, Women, and Biblical Equality" (1989).

3. Council on Biblical Manhood and Womanhood, "Danvers Statement."

4. David M. Scholer, "The Evangelical Debate over Biblical 'Headship'," in *Women, Abuse, and the Bible: How Scripture Can Be Used to Hurt or Heal*, ed. Catherine Clark Kroeger and James R. Beck (Grand Rapids: Baker, 1996), p. 51.

been careful to treat those of opposing viewpoints as sincere fellow believers with whom civil debate should take place.

Moreover, Bill McCartney notwithstanding, Promise Keepers as an organization does not have an official stance on male headship. They recognize that this is an issue about which evangelicals with an equally high view of the Bible can legitimately disagree, and thus do not require their speakers or writers to adhere to a particular party line on the matter. Hence the mixed messages on headship that seem to emanate from Promise Keepers' books and gatherings: each writer and lecturer is giving his own point of view. And while most seem to endorse a form of benign male family headship, there are some in the Promise Keepers organization who take a stance close to that of Christians for Biblical Equality.

So belief in male headship — at least headship in the home, and at least among evangelical groups — is not a confessional issue. But this still leaves people — including members of the press who are doing their best to understand religious currents in contemporary society — wanting to know just *how* one position or the other is defended by an appeal to the Bible. I can recall the frustration of a *Washington Post* reporter who, in light of Promise Keepers' mixed messages on male family headship, finally asked me during a lengthy telephone exchange, "Well, what do *you* do with Ephesians 5:22?" Found in what is called the apostle Paul's "household code," Ephesians 5:22 is the verse (beloved of gender traditionalists) that enjoins wives to be subject to their husbands as to the Lord. As a Christian feminist in the Reformed tradition, I saw this question as an opportunity to plant the outline of biblical egalitarianism in her mind for future journalistic reference.[5] So I took a deep Calvinist breath and said, "If you want to get a biblical perspective on gender relations, you don't start with the Pauline epistles; you start with creation."

Now, believe it or not, starting with creation does not always happen even among evangelicals who claim a high view of the Bible. It is still not unusual to find evangelicals who carry around only a New Testament, or who do carry around a full Bible, but with the words attributed to Jesus printed in red. Each of these practices is, of course, mak-

5. For a more detailed analysis, see Mary Stewart Van Leeuwen, *Gender and Grace: Love, Work, and Parenting in a Changing World* (Downers Grove, Ill.: Intervarsity, 1990).

ing a hermeneutical statement: the first to the effect that the Hebrew Scriptures are at best the background to the doctrinally salient New Testament, and the second to the effect that, in matters of doctrinal or ethical dispute, the words attributed to Jesus trump all other parts of Scripture. Moreover, given the legacy of the fundamentalist-modernist controversy earlier in this century, we still have to cope with the residual tendency of some evangelicals to treat the Bible as "flat book" — as an encyclopedic collection of decontextualized, propositional statements, all of which are either historically or scientifically literal. Ironically, while claiming to challenge "godless science" with a high view of Scripture, fundamentalists have allowed the positivist epistemology of modern science to dictate the terms of the debate — that is, to presume that truth, in Scripture or anywhere else, can only come packaged in scientifically or historically literalist forms.[6]

The result, in the debate about male headship, is a tendency to play what might be called "proof text poker." Traditionalists and egalitarians confront one another with their favorite handful of biblical texts (e.g., Gen. 3:16, Eph. 5:22, 1 Cor. 11:3-10, and Titus 2:5 for traditionalists; Gen. 1:26-28, Job 42:15, Acts 2:17-18, and Gal. 3:28 for egalitarians). The assumption is that the one with the fullest hand of texts wins the argument. This crude hermeneutic, while claiming to represent the highest possible view of Scripture, actually betrays a very low view, for it assumes that we can impose upon the Bible our modernist epistemology with its reverence for "factoids," instead of letting the Bible tell *us* how its various genres and its redemptive-historical flow embody God's truth — a truth which is not to be confused with limited, scientistic notions of inerrancy.

As N. T. Wright suggests,[7] we need to understand the Bible — and thus the story of gender relations within it — as the account of a cosmic drama still in progress. Wright invites us to do the following thought experiment: Consider a troupe of Shakespearean actors, thoroughly versed in Shakespeare's available works, who stumble upon a previously unknown play by the bard. The manuscript includes three acts and the

---

6. Willard M. Swartley, *Slavery, Sabbath, War, and Women: Case Studies in Biblical Interpretation* (Scottsdale, Pa.: Herald, 1983).

7. N. T. Wright, *The New Testament and the People of God* (Minneapolis: Fortress, 1992).

tail end of the fourth act, but the rest of the fourth act is missing. The troupe does know, therefore, how the drama will ultimately end; it knows that in the end the play is a comedy, with a happy ending, and not a tragedy. But to perform the play, the actors must improvise the missing portion of the fourth act, drawing on their knowledge of the rest of the play, on enduring themes and dramatic devices in Shakespeare's other plays, and on what they have learned by working with all these over the course of their individual and corporate acting careers.

So too the Bible reveals a cosmic drama of which God is the ultimate author — a "comedy" with a happy ending for creation and God's people. Creation, fall, redemption, and future hope are the acts of that drama, and we men and women are the actors — made in God's image and called to help bring in God's kingdom — filling in what happens. This we do either more or less in conformity with the Author's purposes, from the resurrection climax at the end of Act 3 to the promise of the new heaven and the new earth that is presented as the fragmentary end of Act 4.

That cosmic drama is for the most part concerned with persons as generic human beings. But there is a subplot concerning gender relations, and it begins with what Reformed theologians have called the "cultural mandate" in the first act of creation. God creates humankind in God's image:

> in the image of God he created them; male and female he created them. God blessed them, and God said to them, "Be fruitful and multiply, and fill the earth and subdue it; and have dominion over the fish of the sea and over the birds of the air and over every living thing that moves upon the earth." (Gen. 1:27-28)

Whatever else we may argue regarding the meaning of "the image of God" from this and other passages, it seems clear that *accountable dominion* or stewardship over the earth is part of that image. The second creation account affirms this when it speaks of God putting the first man in the garden "to till it and keep it" (Gen. 2:15) and to name the animals (Gen. 2:19). Nor is there any indication in the creation accounts that the man was to take the lead in this process. Gender traditionalists have argued in the past that God's making Eve a "helper" fit for Adam (Gen. 2:18) places her in a subordinate position with regard to the cultural mandate. But this is an argument which careful biblical scholarship challenges, for the word for "helper" as used in Genesis 2 is overwhelmingly used elsewhere in the Hebrew Scriptures for the person of God. Yet no Christian would suggest that when we speak of God as "our help" we are making God secondary to ourselves — quite the contrary. Nor does this interpretation argue for the woman's superiority. She is, in Phyllis Trible's translation, the "helper corresponding to the man," one who can walk beside him and work together with him because she is like him in every essential, God-imaging way.[8]

The cultural mandate of Genesis 1:26-28 also shows that accountable sociability — the call to form families and communities within and across generations — is part of the image of God. Note well: God does *not* say to the woman, "Be fruitful and multiply," and to the man, "Subdue the earth." Both mandates are given to both members of the primal pair. This suggests, among other things, that any construction of gender relations that involves an exaggerated separation of the cultural mandate by sex — such as the nineteenth-century doctrine of separate spheres, according to which women were to be "angels of the home" and men "captains of industry" — is eventually going to run into trouble because it is creationally unrealistic and therefore potentially unjust toward both sexes.

Let me point out that I do not think that the doctrine of separate spheres was a nefarious patriarchal plot aimed at keeping women barefoot, pregnant, and in the kitchen. It was, for the most part, a well-intentioned response to the challenges of the industrial revolution. Moreover, it redefined marriage as a primarily companionate endeavor and gave women, perhaps for the first time in history, an arena in which it was assumed (however unrealistically) that they were men's moral superiors. Both these attitudes helped slowly to undermine whatever formal patriarchalism remained at the legal and socioeconomic levels. But, like all social experiments, the doctrine of separate spheres was subject to the law of unintended consequences, and eventually its overdrawn division of the cultural mandate — which, recall, is a *human,* not a *gendered,* mandate — resulted in the first and second waves of feminism.

Interestingly, when my female African-American students discuss

---

8. Phyllis Trible, *God and the Rhetoric of Sexuality* (Philadelphia: Fortress, 1978).

these issues, they often point out (if I haven't done so already) that the actual practice of separate spheres was available almost exclusively to economically privileged whites, and that their own grandmothers did not even have the choice to be bored in suburbia. They are rightly angry at the economic discrimination that forced their mothers (and often their fathers) to work a "double day," but they are happy — often proud — that their ethnic legacy is one that, for the most part, did not divide the cultural mandate by sex.

Much ink has been spilled by Christians throughout history regarding Act 2 of the biblical drama — the narrative of the fall of humankind and its implications for relations between men and women. Augustine, Aquinas, and Luther (but not Calvin) all claimed that male headship was justified by the fact that women were responsible for the fall into sin. But responsible exegetes of both sexes see Genesis 3:16 ("your desire shall be for your husband, and he shall rule over you") as *descriptive* of the tragic consequences of the fall, not *prescriptive* — and certainly not to be read back into creation. Some feminist exegetes have gone a step further, saying that this passage suggests a differential "fallout of the fall" on men and women. In light of the fall, men are more likely to distort the cultural mandate by turning accountable dominion into *domination* — of other people and of the rest of creation. By contrast, women are tempted to turn the call to accountable sociability into *social enmeshment* — that is, to use the preservation of existing relationships (however unjust or unhealthy) as an excuse *not* to exercise accountable dominion as imagers of God.[9]

This is not to say that that the positive, mutual interdependence that existed between man and woman at creation has totally disappeared; humans are still made in God's image, even though this image is distorted. Nevertheless, Genesis 3:15 seems to be saying that as a result of the fall there will be a propensity in men to let their dominion run wild — to impose it in cavalier and illegitimate ways not only on the earth and on other men but also on the helper. Legitimate, accountable dominion all too easily becomes male domination. And the woman's analogue of the man's congenital flaw, in light of Genesis 3:16, is the temptation to avoid taking risks — to avoid exercising legitimate dominion — if such

---

9. Judith Plaskow, *Sex, Sin, and Grace* (Washington, D.C.: University Press of America, 1980); Van Leeuwen, *Gender and Grace*.

risks would upset existing relationships. It is the temptation to let creational sociability become distorted social enmeshment. Thus, the kind of essentialism that says that men, either naturally or by divine fiat, are to be "aggressive" (or at least more assertive) and that women are to be "passive" (or at least much less assertive) not only carelessly bifurcates the cultural mandate but also panders to the worst impulses of our fallen natures. On this reading, to recapture a responsible rendering of the image of God, men may often need to be *less* assertive and women *more*.

With regard to the third or redemptive act of the drama, biblical egalitarians not only focus on what St. Paul said but on what Jesus himself did in his relationships with women. He included them among his followers, spoke to them in public, touched them when they were deemed ritually unclean, and insisted on restoring a high standard of monogamy for women and men alike. He also proclaimed to a culture obsessed with blood ties (and in which barren women were a disgrace) that the family of God was so much more important that it might even divide parents and children. This, according to biblical egalitarians, points to a redeemed vision for relations between men and women in which justice, righteousness, and a right recovery of the cultural mandate prevail.

And what about all those Pauline passages (including Eph. 5:22) that seem to endorse women's silence in the churches and male headship in the family? These must be put alongside all the other passages in which Paul praises female leaders of house churches, gives instructions for how women should in fact speak in church, and commends one woman for helping straighten out the doctrinal confusions of a male colleague. And while using the language of wifely submission in some places, Paul reminds his readers in other places that spouses' bodies belong equally to each other and that husbands are to be ready to sacrifice, like Christ, unto death for their wives. Paul's mixed voices on this issue would seem to indicate that he supports women's freedom in Christ but that, for the sake of spreading the gospel, he does not want women to let their freedom go to their heads. In the midst of a patriarchal society already inclined to see this new Jewish-messianic sect as at best somewhat weird and at worst subversive of the political order, some concessions to local gender norms were essential.[10]

10. Craig S. Keener, *Paul, Women, and Wives: Marriage and Women's Ministry in the Letters of Paul* (Peabody, Mass.: Hendrickson, 1992).

The analogy with slavery is instructive. Just as Paul does not call for the sudden overturning by Christians of slavery as an institution, but undermines it from within by urging both slaves and masters to treat each other as brothers in Christ, so too for the sake of social order and successful evangelism he advises the recipients of his letters to play along with some of the local norms of patriarchy even as he proclaims that in Christ "There is no longer Jew or Greek, there is no longer slave or free, there is no longer male and female; for all of you are one in Christ Jesus" (Gal. 3:28). In each case, as we live out and fill in the central parts of Act 4 of the biblical drama — what theologian Oscar Cullman called the time "between D-Day and V-Day" or the time of "the already but the not yet" — the redemptive-historical line we must travel seems clear. The barriers between Jew and Gentile, slave and free, male and female are to come down, and we are together to be "heirs of the gracious gift of life" (1 Peter 3:7).

The above analysis in no way implies that only married human couples can image God and carry out the cultural mandate adequately. It is useful to think of the Christian life as a series of "offices" or vocations that nest inside each other like the boxes of a child's stacking toy. The overriding office of all Christians, whether men or women, is that of redeemed sinner, committed to building God's kingdom of justice and peace as members of Christ's body. Within that box are smaller boxes. Thus, that we are women and men created to express mutuality is important, but not of supreme importance; the goals of the kingdom contain and override it. That God calls some people to marriage is also part of the creation order and the kingdom order — a box within the larger boxes. But again, it is not of supreme importance; the goals of the kingdom contain and override it. That is why Paul can affirm the goodness of marriage, yet praise the office of singleness for the greater freedom it gives for kingdom work (1 Cor. 7:25-39).

Finally, it also needs to be said that biblical equal regard does not require the endorsement of undifferentiated androgyny. The cultural mandate is God's call to practice "freedom within form" — that is, the opening up of the rich potential of creation within the limits set by God. Gender is never a completely social construction. At the very least, it must cooperate with the physical and reproductive differences between the sexes as these interact with the eco-cultural setting in which a group lives. This means that what constitutes fairness and equality in gender relations will necessarily be somewhat different in a subsistence hunting and gathering society than in an agricultural society, and the latter still different from a post-industrial society. Indeed, within a given family in any culture, gender justice will take different forms at different stages of the family life cycle. But when you add to this individual differences that have nothing to do with sex — the "varieties of gifts, but the same Spirit" of which Paul wrote (1 Cor. 12:4) — then we have little mandate for laying down rigid, let alone hierarchical, gender scripts. Within the biblical norms of fidelity, mutual regard, and commitment to rearing the next generation to healthy maturity, there is more than one way faithfully to play out the last act of the biblical drama.

CHAPTER 3

Did Early Christians Teach, or Merely Assume, Male Headship?

Carolyn Osiek

MY TOPIC reminds me of two encounters. The first was with a group of family friends. When I posed the question of whether Christianity teaches male headship, all three immediately said yes; one woman described being raised to leave always the best or the last of everything "for the men," who would repay in kindness. In the second encounter, a woman friend who takes religion seriously responded, "What is male headship?" That the first respondent was Protestant, the second Catholic, may be relevant, but I give the two examples to show that there are varieties of approaches and varieties of perceptions, and that "headship" is not necessarily at the top of everyone's mind.

We must all be aware when discussing such a topic that there is also a problem of interpretation. If we do not agree on an interpretive tradition and method, we will not agree about the meaning of specific texts. This problem is certainly at issue here.

Does the Bible teach male headship? I would certainly say it presumes male headship. References to individuals as "head" (*rosh*, Hebrew, or *kephale*, Greek) are quite common in biblical and other ancient sources, and of the numerous examples, they are nearly always male: a military commander, a chief of a clan, a ruler, or the leader of a group of people. This metaphorical use of the word for "head" tells us that the people of ancient biblical times considered the anatomical head as the guiding agent of the human body. The metaphor or comparison does not work without another implied or expressed metaphor, that of "body." Thus, when an individual man is the "head" of a group, it is implied that the group is the "body." So the metaphor of body and head, applied to a social body and its leader, is already in place well before Paul.

More recently, the argument has been put forth that *kephale* (head) can mean "source" rather than "leader," particularly in the case of 1 Corinthians 11:3, where Paul says that the head of the man is Christ, the head of the woman is the man, and the head of Christ is God. There is some good evidence for interpreting *kephale* as "source" here, but I think the critics are correct that most of the evidence does not support that interpretation as a general meaning. What few people notice, however, is the very unusual way in which "head" is used in 1 Corinthians 11:3, as leader or authority of one person over *one other person*. This is very rare outside the Pauline letters, possibly even unknown, and may suggest a different meaning. What we are talking about here is headship very narrowly defined as leadership or authority of one man over one woman, specifically in marriage.

Only two biblical passages talk about male dominance over a woman using the language of headship, 1 Corinthians 11:3 and Ephesians 5:23. The other two household code passages, Colossians 3:18 and 1 Peter 3:1, do not use the language of headship, but rather the very different language of submission. Ephesians 5:21-33, on which we will focus in this essay, compares the headship of husband over wife with that of Christ over the church through an analogy: the husband is the head of his wife as Christ is the head of his body, the church. The analogy only works if the woman is equated with the "body," so that male headship corresponds to the headship of Christ over his "body," the church. Since the analogy of head and body is, as we have noted, normally applied to the position of one man over a group of people, it is used traditionally in the case of Christ and his church. In the case of husband and wife, where one person is described as the head of another, the comparison is not at all traditional.

It would seem that the author of Ephesians has come to this analogy in the following way: In different passages of 1 Corinthians, man is head of woman (11:3) and the church is Christ's body (12:12-27), although the head is not mentioned. Colossians 1:18 adds to the church/body metaphor that Christ is head of his body the church (cf. also Eph. 1:22; 2:16; 3:6; 4:15). There is no distinction in Greek between the words "man" and "husband" (both are rendered by *aner*) nor between "woman" and "wife" (both are rendered by *gyne*). Now Christ is the head of his body/church, and a husband is the head of his body/wife. All the author of Ephesians has to do, then, is to combine the two metaphors into one analogy: a husband is the head of his wife as Christ is the head of the church.

Ancient Greek writings on household management typically portray the paterfamilias, the male householder, as one who rules in different ways over his wife, children, and slaves. He also receives instruction on financial management. In the New Testament household codes, however, including this passage in Ephesians, that last part has disappeared, and other differences from the typical pattern emerge: subordinate members are not only addressed but addressed first; they are granted a personal dignity that they do not possess in previous discussions. The center of attention has shifted from the husband/father/master — who is now encouraged to treat all of his charges with love and gentleness — to the mutual relationships among household members. All of these changes occur because the discussion is no longer about household management but about family relationships.

The Ephesians passage is not primarily about marriage, however, but about the church, as is the whole epistle, whose major theme is the reconciliation of Jewish and Gentile Christians in their common faith in Christ. There are at least four different ways to read the purpose of Ephesians 5:21-33:

1. It is primarily intended for the education of social inferiors, wives, children, and slaves, teaching them how to submit to their paterfamilias, or male authority. (Although it can be read this way, I think there is clearly more going on than that.)

2. It is primarily education for males in how to become self-sacrificing, an education that seems to be repeated with some regularity in Christian teaching and to fascinate males because so much of their socialization is in the opposite direction, toward self-centeredness for success. Examples include the thesis of Caroline Walker Bynum that the medieval monastic devotion to Jesus as mother and the abbot as mother were a way for males to express humility and gentleness, both qualities identified with females.[1] Another example is Reinhold Niebuhr's proposal of pride as the original sin, which seems to work for men but not for women.[2]

1. Caroline Walker Bynum, *Jesus As Mother: Studies in the Spirituality of the High Middle Ages* (Berkeley: University of California Press, 1982).
2. See Valerie Saiving Goldstein, "The Human Situation: A Feminine View," *Journal of Religion* 40 (1960): 100-112.

3. It holds up wives (and to a lesser extent, children and slaves) as normative Christians, all of whom are to submit to each other (v. 21) after the manner of 1 Peter 2:18-25, which holds up Christian slaves as normative Christians for suffering unjustly.

4. It is primarily a new set of insights about the church arising from the traditional household code. It combines traditions of sacred marriage and biblical spousal relationships between God and Israel. The wife-husband relationship is accidental, providing only the starting point for the reflection about the church based on a familiar patriarchal pattern.

All but the first alternative hold rich possibilities, and the argument is not about whether Christianity introduced new and liberating trends. That discussion nearly always ends by being anti-Jewish in its argument that Jesus freed social inferiors from Jewish oppression.

Examination of the historical context shows clearly that something new was happening in the first century in thinking and practice about male-female marriage relationships, among both non-Christians and Christians. For instance, the Roman Stoic philosopher Musonius Rufus urges the same education for women as for men and opposes a double standard about marital fidelity. The Roman writers Cornelius Nepos and Valerius Maximus tell us that Roman women were now reclining next to their husbands on banquet couches, a custom never before practiced by "respectable" women. While the legal practice of *tutela* or male guardianship over women's business transactions was still in force, the emperor Augustus offered at a time of low birth rates to waive it for any freeborn woman who produced three children, and any freedwoman who produced four, and Claudius later abolished the practice. Plutarch's marriage advice contains some very patriarchal ideas about a husband's control over the life of his wife, so that, for example, she should at marriage leave her own family gods and worship only his, yet he could also talk about marriage as friendship between husband and wife, which was not the usual way that it was thought of by the elite.[3]

The New Testament household codes follow this trend and take a

---

3. Further information can be found in Carolyn Osiek and David Balch, *Families in the New Testament World: Households and House Churches* (Louisville: Westminster/John Knox, 1997), pp. 57-60.

bold step forward by placing wives, children, and slaves ahead of husbands, fathers, and masters in their portrayal of the Christian family. The best way to be faithful to a biblical vision is to do what they did, to continue the early Christian movement toward something like what Don Browning and others call "equal regard." In today's world, anything less than equal regard fails to acknowledge the full personhood of women. An overly literal interpretation of any biblical text out of context can lead to an impoverishment of symbols. An over-identification of the analogy of the husband as head of wife and Christ as head of church is no exception. When a symbol or metaphor becomes fixed and no longer points beyond itself, it loses its power to reveal the mystery of God. I fully support the renewal of fatherhood and fatherly responsibility. I do not believe that it must be at the expense of women.

CHAPTER 4

Male Headship:
Reform of the Protestant Tradition

John Witte Jr.

BOTH THE LEGAL and the Protestant traditions of the West have offered multiple answers to the question whether Christianity teaches male headship. The answers change as one moves from medieval Catholic canon law to early modern civil law to twentieth-century Anglo-American common law. The answers change further as one moves across mainline Lutheran, Calvinist, Anglican, and Anabaptist traditions, and as one moves forward within each denomination from the sixteenth century until today. And the answers change again as one moves through institutions of the household, the church, the state, and voluntary associations. In broad historical outline, the theological presumption of male headship is stronger among Calvinists and Anglicans than among Lutherans and Anabaptists, and stronger among sixteenth- and seventeenth-century Protestants than among their modern successors. Also in broad historical outline, the legal presumption of male headship has been more fully maintained within the household and the church, where group identity and rights are more heavily emphasized, than within the state and voluntary associations, where individual rights and equality have higher priority.

Both the theology and the law of the Protestant traditions have had to steer a course between patriarchal monism and gender-blind egalitarianism. Even the most rigid patriarchal models of headship have had to yield to the perennial realities of queenships, matriarchal associations, and single-mother households. Even the most rigorous expositions of gender equality have had to acknowledge the distinct callings and capacities of males and females in the processes of procreation, nurture, and education of children. An emerging theme of the Western Protestant tradition has thus been to emphasize the ontological equality of males and females before God even while differentiating, and sometimes chauvinistically prioritizing, their respective callings and offices. An emerging theme of the Western legal tradition has been to emphasize the constitutional equality of men and women even while allowing churches, households, and other nonstate associations to strike their own internal balances between headship and equality, authority and liberty.

James Fitzjames Stephen versus John Stuart Mill

Rather than tracking this moving picture of male headship with anecdotes, permit me to summarize a vigorous literary debate about male headship within marriage in mid-nineteenth-century England. The antagonists in the debate were James Fitzjames Stephen, a prominent Anglican jurist and moralist, and John Stuart Mill, a leading libertarian and utilitarian. Both were distinguished men of letters and occasional legislators. Both spoke for broad constituencies — Stephen for an old Protestant order featuring marital headship, Mill for a new libertarian order featuring equality between the sexes. The setting for much of their debate was the ferment in Parliament for the reform of the traditional English law of marriage — ferment that found equal force in American state legislatures at the same time. The Stephen-Mill debate was focused by several bills that sought to liberalize marriage and divorce rules, to liberate children from abusive households, and to enhance the rights of wives to their property and minor children. For Stephen, the heart of the debate was over the essential character of marriage and the family: is this institution "a divine, indissoluble union governed by the *paterfamilias* [at its head], or is it a contractual unit governed and dissolved by the wills of the parties?" Speaking for the old order, Stephen defended the first position. "[T]he political and social changes which have taken place in the world since the sixteenth century [Protestant Reformation] have . . . been eminently beneficial to mankind," Stephen wrote. "The terms of the marriage relation as settled by the law and religion of Europe" since the Protestant Reformation must be maintained.[1]

---

1. See James Fitzjames Stephen, *Liberty, Equality, and Fraternity*, ed. Stuart D. Warner (Indianapolis: Liberty Fund, 1993), pp. 15, 138-53; James Fitzjames Stephen, "Mar-

The "settled" *theological* view of Stephen's day was that marriage is a "state of existence ordained by the Creator," "a consummation of the Divine command to multiply and replenish the earth," "the only stable substructure of social, civil, and religious institutions." Marriage was almost universally taken to be a permanent monogamous union between a fit man and woman designed at once for mutual love and affection, mutual procreation and nurture of children, mutual protection from spiritual and civil harms.

The "settled" *legal* view of Stephen's day was that marriage depended for its legitimacy on the absolute and unequivocal consent of both the woman and the man. Marriage formation required formal betrothals, publication of banns, parental consent, peer witnesses, church consecration, and state consecration. Marriages would be annulled, on petition of either party, if couples were related by various blood or family ties identified in the Mosaic law, or where one party proved impotent, frigid, sterile, or had a contagious disease that precluded procreation or endangered the other spouse. Marriages could also be annulled if one of the parties had been coerced, tricked, or misled into marriage.

The "settled" *natural* view of Stephen's day was that men are created with superior power, ability, and opportunity in life, which they must discharge with due restraint and accountability to God. Women have a special calling to be wives and mothers, teachers and nurturers of children, which calling they must discharge in the household. Our law and religion reflect these natural sentiments, said Stephen, "by prescribing monogamy, indissoluble marriage on the footing of the obedience of the wife to the husband, and a division of labour among men and women with corresponding differences in the matters of conduct, manners, and dress."

Nature is defied if marriage is treated as a simple contract, Stephen argued. This notion assumes falsely that men and women are equal. To allow marriage to become "a simple bargained-for contract," without oversight by parents and peers and by church and state, "will inevitably expose women to great abuse." They will have no protection in forming the bargain with naturally superior men, nor protection from men who

---

riage Settlements," *Cornhill Review* (Dec. 1863): 1-6; and James Fitzjames Stephen, "English Jurisprudence," *Edinburgh Review* (Oct. 1861): 456-86.

dismiss them when barren, old, unattractive, troubled, or destitute. "The truth is," Stephen thundered, "that the change of marriage . . . from status to contract" "is not favorable to equality." "Men [and women] are fundamentally unequal, and this inequality will show itself, arrange society [and its law] as you like." "If marriage is to be permanent," and justice and liberty properly guarded, "the government of the family must be put by law and by morals in the hands of the husband."

Nature is also defied if the family is treated as an open contractual society, subject to multiple claims of right by its members. The family, once formed, is an independent institution that "lies at the foundation of both church and state." The husband and father is the head of the family, just as the monarch is the head of church and state. As paterfamilias, he must rule the household as God's vice-regent with all benevolence, grace, and Christian devotion. A wife is the husband's co-helper in the family, a child his ward and agenda, both of whom must obey his every reasonable command.

Stephen was well aware of the potential abuses in this traditional law. "No one," he writes, "contends that a man ought to have power to order his wife and children about like slaves and beat them if they disobey him." Such abusive conduct must be punished severely, he argued, but on a case-by-case basis.

John Stuart Mill attacked Stephen's sentiments with arguments well known in England's liberal circles. Mill's attack was, in part, directed against the abuses allowed by this traditional system of marriage and family law. But Mill's deeper attack was theological — "laying bare the real root of much that is bowed down to as the intention of Nature and the ordinance of God." The prevailing theology and law of marriage and the family supported a "three-fold patriarchy," Mill charged. The church dictates to the state its peculiar understanding of nature. The state dictates to the couple the terms of their marital relation and abandons them once the terms are accepted. The man lords over his wife and children, divesting them of all liberty and license in their person and property, thought and belief.[2]

2. See *Collected Works of John Stuart Mill*, ed. John M. Robson, repr. ed. (Toronto: University of Toronto Press, 1984), 3:952-53; 16:1470; 17:1624, 1668-69, 1692-94; 19:401; 21:37, 46, 261-63, 287-89, 299-322; 23:677-80; 25:1172-76; Ann P. Robson and John M. Robson, eds., *Sexual Equality: Writings by John Stuart Mill, Harriet Taylor Mill, and Helen Taylor* (Toronto: University of Toronto Press, 1994), pp. 23, 28-34, 53-102.

Nature does not teach the headship of man or the subjection of women, said Mill, but "a perfect equality" of spouses. "If marriage were an equal contract . . . and if [a woman] would find all honourable employments as freely open to her as to men," marriages could be true institutions of liberty and affection, shaped by the preferences of wife and husband, not the prescriptions of church and state.

Nature also does not teach tyranny and commodification of children by the paterfamilias. Children are not items of property, to be sold on the market of marriage, or conduits through which to pass the family name and property. Nor are children slaves to be worked and whipped into submission and performance by the paterfamilias. If the family were an open unit, where children could seek redress from neglect, abuse, and arbitrary rule, a real family could be realized and true happiness for all parties involved could be attained. If the paterfamilias does not "fulfill his obligation to feed, nurture, and educate his child with love and patience," said Mill, the *paterpoliticus,* the state as the child's protector under the social contract, "ought to see it fulfilled, at the charge, as far as possible, of the parent."

Legal Reforms

Mill's critique anticipated many of the reforms of Anglo-American marriage law enacted over the next 150 years.[3] The reforms came in two waves. The first wave, which broke slowly over England and America from the mid-nineteenth to the mid-twentieth centuries, was designed to bring greater equality and equity to the traditional household, without necessarily denying the traditional Christian ideals of marriage that had helped to form this institution. The second wave of reform, which has been breaking in America since the early 1960s, seems calcu-

3. See sources and discussion in R. H. Graveson and F. R. Crane, eds., *A Century of Family Law: 1857-1957* (London: Sweet and Maxwell, 1957); Max Rheinstein, *Marriage Stability, Divorce, and the Law* (Chicago: University of Chicago Press, 1972); Mary Lyndon Shanley, *Feminism, Marriage, and the Law in Victorian England, 1850-1895* (Princeton, N.J.: Princeton University Press, 1989); Susan Staves, *Married Women's Separate Property in England, 1660-1833* (Cambridge: Harvard University Press, 1990); Lawrence Stone, *Road to Divorce: A History of the Making and Breaking of Marriage in England* (New York: Oxford University Press, 1995).

lated to break the preeminence of traditional family law, and the basic Christian values that once sustained it.

The first wave of legal reforms brought greater protection to women and children. New legislation released married women from the legal bonds of "coverture," which traditionally had subsumed a married woman's person and property into that of her husband. A married woman could now hold independent title and control, and exercise independent contractual and testimonial rights, over the property she brought into the marriage or acquired thereafter. She also gained the capacity to litigate in respect of her property, without intermeddling by her husband. As their rights to property were enhanced, (married) women slowly gained broader rights to higher education, learned societies, trade and commercial guilds and unions, and various professions, occupations, societies, and the franchise — all of which had been largely closed to them.

Other new legislation provided that, in cases of annulment or divorce, courts had discretion to place minor children in the custody of that parent who was best suited to care for them. This reversed the traditional presumption that child custody belonged to the father. The wife could now claim custody, particularly where children were of tender years or where the husband was found to be cruel, abusive, or unfit as a caretaker. Courts retained the traditional power to order guilty husbands to pay alimony to innocent wives, and were newly empowered to make other "reasonable" allocations of marital property to the innocent wife for child support.

These and other early reforms sought to improve traditional marriage lore and law more than to abandon it. Most of these reformers, Mill among them, accepted the Christian ideal of marriage as a permanent union of a fit man and woman of the age of consent. Most accepted the classic Augustinian definition of the marital goods of *fides, proles, et sacramentum* — sacrificial love, supportive procreation, and symbolic stability. The primary goal of these early reformers was to purge the household of the paternalism and patriarchy inherent in some traditional views of headship, and thus to render the ideals of marriage a greater reality for all.

The legal reforms introduced during this first phase were designed to render marriages easier to contract, maintain, and dissolve. Courts were more deferential to the wishes of both marital parties —

before, during, and after their wedding. Wives received greater protections from their husbands and greater independence in their relationships outside the household. Children received greater protection from parental abuse and greater access to benefit rights. Young women, in particular, received greater freedom to forgo or postpone marriage, and greater social, political, and economic opportunities, regardless of their marital status. While traditionally a woman's consent was considered essential only for purposes of marital formation, now it was becoming essential to all phases of the marital process. While traditionally male headship was considered the natural condition of a voluntarily formed marriage, it was increasingly viewed as a negotiable term, particularly if the woman or her family had ample political or economic power.

It should be noted that this transformation of marital headship was as much a reformation as a rejection of basic Protestant lore. One goal of the sixteenth-century Protestant Reformers had been to remove the cleric as a mediator between God and the laity — following St. Peter's teaching on the priesthood of all believers. One consequence of embracing the principle of headship was to interpose the paterfamilias as a mediator between God and his wife — following St. Paul's teaching on household codes. Later Protestants slowly parsed this tension by reemphasizing classic Protestant themes of the equality of men and women in Christ, and of their respective vocations before God.

Since the early 1960s, American reformers have taken the lead in pressing the Enlightenment contractarian model of marriage to the more radical conclusions that Mill and others had intimated. The same Enlightenment ideals of liberty and equality which had earlier driven reforms of traditional marriage laws have come to be used to reject these laws altogether. The traditional Christian ideal of marriage as a permanent spiritual union designed for the sake of mutual love, procreation, and protection is slowly giving way to a new reality of marriage as a terminal sexual contract designed for the gratification of the individual parties.

Today, John Stuart Mill's contractual ideal of marriage as "a private, bargained-for exchange between husband and wife about all their rights, goods, and interests" has become a legal reality in America. The strong presumption today is that adult parties have free entrance into marital contracts, free exercise of marital relationships, and free exit from marriages once their contractual obligations are discharged. Antenuptial, marital, and separation contracts that allow parties to define their own rights and duties within the marital estate and thereafter have gained increasing acceptance. Implied marital contracts are imputed to longstanding lovers. Surrogacy contracts are executed for the rental of wombs. Medical contracts are executed for the abortion of fetuses. Traditional requirements of parental consent, peer witness, church consecration, or civil registration for all these contracts have largely disappeared. No-fault unilateral divorce statutes have reduced the divorce proceeding to an expensive formality. Lump sum property exchanges now often substitute for alimony. Parties are still bound to continue to support their minor children, within and without marriage; but this merely expresses another contractual principle — that parties respect the reliance and expectation interests of their children, who are third-party beneficiaries of their parents' marital or sexual contracts.

Today, however, James Fitzjames Stephen's warning that undue contractualization of marriage would bring ruin to many women and children has also become a social reality in America. Premarital, marital, separation, and divorce contracts too often are not arms-length transactions, and too often are not driven by rational calculus alone. In the heady romance of budding nuptials, parties are often blind to the full consequences of their bargain. In the emotional anguish of separation and divorce, parties can be driven more by the desire for short-term relief from the other spouse than by the concern for their long-term welfare or that of their children. The economically stronger and more calculating spouse triumphs in these contexts. And in the majority of cases today, that party is still the man — despite the loud egalitarian rhetoric to the contrary.

"Underneath the mantle of equality that has been draped over the ongoing family, the state of nature flourishes," Mary Ann Glendon writes.[4] In this state of nature, freedom and privacy reign supreme. But married life is becoming increasingly "brutish, nasty, and short" — with women and children bearing the primary costs. Recall the familiar statistics: In the 1990s, a quarter of all pregnancies were aborted. A third

4. Mary Ann Glendon, *The Transformation of Family Law: State, Law, and Family in the United States and Western Europe* (Chicago: University of Chicago Press, 1989), p. 146.

of all children were born to single mothers. One-half of all marriages ended in divorce. Two-thirds of all black children lived apart from their fathers. The number of "lost children" in America was more than fifteen million. The greater the repeal of regulation of marriage for the sake of marital freedom and sexual privacy, the greater the threat to real freedom for women and children. The very contractarian gospel that first promised salvation from the abuses of earlier Christian models of marriage and headship now threatens with even graver abuse.

Lessons from the Tradition

What is the way out of this dilemma? There have been, and must be, many responses.[5] Mine is the expected response of a historian: "Back to the sources!" — but now newly enlightened. The achievements of the Enlightenment in reforming the theology and law of marriage cannot be lost on us. It took the contractual radicalism of Mill and his contemporaries to force the Western tradition to reform itself — to grant greater respect to the rights of women and children, to break the monopoly and monotony of outmoded moral and religious forms and forums respecting sexuality, marriage, and the family, to purge the excesses born of traditional understandings of male headship. Some religious traditions may have retrieved or conceived their own resources to achieve these reforms, but it was the Enlightenment critique that forced these traditions to reform themselves and the state to reform its laws. This was no small achievement.

Just as the Enlightenment tradition still has much to teach us today, so do the earlier Protestant traditions. Protestants have seen that marriages are at once natural, spiritual, social, and contractual units; that in order to survive and flourish, this institution must be governed both externally by legal authorities and internally by moral authorities. Protestants have seen that the household is an inherently communal enterprise, in which marital couples, magistrates, and ministers must all inevitably cooperate to achieve the marital goods of mutual love,

---

5. See the monumental efforts in Don S. Browning et al., *From Culture Wars to Common Ground: Religion and the American Family Debate* (Louisville: Westminster/John Knox, 1997).

mutual procreation, and mutual protection of a person from sexual sin.

One modern lesson in this is that we must resist the temptation to reduce marriage to a single perspective or to a single authority. A single perspective on marriage — whether religious, social, or contractual — does not capture the full nuance of marriage. A single authority over marriage — whether the church, state, or paterfamilias — is not fully competent to govern all marital questions. Marriage demands multiple perspectives and multiple authorities to be understood and governed adequately.

A second lesson is that we must resist looking to the state alone for the sources of our marriage law. American religious communities need to think much more seriously about restoring and reforming their own bodies of religious law on marriage, divorce, and sexuality, instead of simply acquiescing in state laws. American states, in turn, must think more seriously about granting greater deference to the marital laws and customs of legitimate religious and cultural groups, with the state setting only minimum conditions to facilitate such unions and criminal law limits against abuses of wives and children. The introduction of such legal pluralism might well lead some Christian, Jewish, Muslim, and other religious groups to reinstitute traditional forms of headship within the household. American Baptist churches have made headlines of late by announcing such a position. But if a religious community mandates responsible male — or female — headship as a condition for voluntary membership in the religious community, or for holding distinctive offices or powers within it, a state that respects religious freedom ultimately has little constitutional ground to object. So long as membership in such religious communities, and their constituent household units, remains voluntary, and parties commit no threats or violence to life and limb to their members, the rights of the religious group to define its ideal marital forms must trump.

A promising recent development, which builds on the lessons of both the Protestant and Enlightenment traditions, is the rise of covenant marriage laws. Such laws were first enacted in Louisiana in 1997, and are now under consideration in several other states. Under these laws, marrying couples may choose either a traditional contract marriage with attendant rights to no-fault divorce, or a covenant marriage, with more stringent formation and dissolution rules. In forming a covenant marriage, the parties must receive detailed counseling from a licensed therapist or religious official, read the entire covenant marriage statute, and then swear an oath, pledging "full knowledge of the nature, purposes, and responsibilities of marriage" and promising "to love, honor, and care for one another as husband and wife for the rest of [their] lives." Divorce is allowed such covenanted couples only on proof of adultery, capital felony, malicious desertion or separation for more than a year, and/or physical or sexual abuse of the spouse or one of the children. Formal separation is allowed on any of these grounds, as well as on proof of habitual intemperance, cruel treatment, or outrages of the other spouse.[6]

This is a cleverly drawn statute that seeks to respect both the inherent virtues of contractual calculus, emphasized by the Enlightenment tradition, and the inherent goods of marital union, emphasized by the Protestant tradition. The statute has been attacked, predictably, as an encroachment on sexual freedom and the rights of women and children, as a "Trojan horse" to smuggle biblical principles into American law, and as a throwback to the days of staged and spurious charges of marital infidelity which "no fault" statutes sought to overcome. But, given the neutral language of the statute and its explicit protections of both voluntary entrance and involuntary exit from the covenant union, such objections are largely inapt. The statute should help to inject both a greater level of realism into the heady romance of prospective couples and a greater level of rigor into the state's law of marriage formation and dissolution.

The stronger objection to the Louisiana statute is not that it jeopardizes liberty but that it trivializes covenant. The statute effectively reduces "covenant" to a super marriage contract between the husband and wife alone. Historically, however, marriage covenants involved parents, peers, ministers, and magistrates as well, who served at least as checks on each other and the prospective couple, if not as representatives of God in the covenant formation. Indeed, according to classic Protestant theology, the couple's parents, as God's bishops for children, gave their consent to the union. Two parties, as God's priests to

---

6. See sources and discussion in John Witte Jr. et al., eds., *Covenant Marriage in Comparative Perspectives* (Grand Rapids: Wm. B. Eerdmans, forthcoming).

their peers, served as witnesses to the marriage. The minister, holding God's spiritual power of the Word, blessed the couple and admonished them in their spiritual duties. The magistrate, holding God's temporal power of the sword, registered the parties and their properties and ensured the legality of their union. These four parties represented different dimensions of God's involvement in the marriage covenant, and were thus essential to the legitimacy of the marriage covenant itself.[7] The Louisiana law replaces all four of these parties with a licensed marriage counselor. Moreover, it leaves it to the state to decide the terms of the marital covenant, the credentials of the marriage counselor, the contents of the marriage oath. Historically, however, churches and synagogues defined these matters for themselves, without much state interference. Perhaps this covenant statute will be the first step toward a more embracive legal pluralism — one that respects the rights of individuals and religious groups to devise their own institutions of liberty and authority, equality and headship.

7. See Max L. Stackhouse, *Covenant and Commitments: Faith, Family, and Economic Life* (Louisville: Westminster/John Knox, 1997); and John Witte Jr., *From Sacrament to Contract: Marriage, Religion, and Law in the Western Tradition* (Louisville: Westminster/John Knox, 1997), chap. 3.

CHAPTER 5

The Feminist Pope

Lisa Sowle Cahill

DOES CHRISTIANITY teach male headship? Not according to the pope. John Paul II does not assert the authority of men over women in the family. Instead, he uses categories evoking equality, equal dignity, reciprocity, and mutuality to describe the relation of spouses. A favorite description of the ideal spousal relationship is "mutual self-gift."

In February 1998, I had the occasion to attend a papal audience at the Vatican after participating in an international, Vatican-sponsored conference on "Women's Health Issues." Having completed his prepared remarks to our group, John Paul II stood up, pointed to himself, and repeated twice, "Papa feminista!" (The feminist pope!) His tone and expression were grandfatherly and even jocular, and this pontifical self-description elicited chuckles from the two hundred or so conference attendees. All found it surprising, some enigmatic, and many incredible.[1] But the apparent desire of John Paul II to style himself a defender of feminist aspirations is not impossible, given several of his previous statements on women's status.

In his 1981 treatise *On the Family,* John Paul II insists, "It is important to underline the equal dignity and responsibility of women with men." He explains that "this equality is realized in a unique manner in that reciprocal self-giving by each to the other and by both to the children which is proper to marriage and the family."[2] In a letter written in

1. For some further reflections on this rather surprising incident, by another conference attendee, see Sidney Callahan, "The Feminist Pope: But Who Does the Dishes?" *Commonweal* 125, no. 7 (1998): 7-8.

2. John Paul II, *On the Family* (Washington, D.C.: United States Catholic Conference, 1981), no. 22.

1995, preparing the for United Nations' Fourth World Conference on Women in Beijing, the pope notes past and present injustices to women. He expresses admiration for women who have fought for "their basic social, economic and political rights," even in times when this was considered "a lack of femininity, a manifestation of exhibitionism, and even a sin!" He refers to "the great process of women's liberation," and voices regret that women are still often not "acknowledged, respected and appreciated."[3]

It may be true, as many feminist theologians have pointed out, that the ideal of male-female equality is undermined by the pope's insistence that motherhood is the primary feminine vocation, and by the exclusion of women from priestly ministry. It is also just as true, however, that John Paul II has defended the equality and rights of women in the family and in society to an extent far exceeding the teaching of previous pontiffs.

There are at least three factors that explain the pope's position on women and his nonendorsement of a "headship" model of the family. First, it should be noted that he does not favor a liberal feminism, focused on autonomy. Rather, in accord with Catholic social teaching, he adopts a social view of the person. In this view, all have a right to share equally in the common good, but rights and duties are reciprocal and interdependent. Also, different roles can be appropriate for different people without violating the basic principle of equality. Regarding women, John Paul II sees motherhood as their special role, without granting that this places women in a submissive position in relation to men. Second, and related to this, is the pope's strong "preferential option for the poor," an approach to social ethics in which the vulnerable and marginalized are given special attention. In many cultures of the world, and in some aspects of all societies, it is taken for granted that women are the social inferiors of men, and hence they are deprived of full participation in the common good. For this reason the pope advocates for women's dignity, along with that of other vulnerable groups.

Third, the Catholic approach to theology and conduct has never

3. John Paul II, *Letter to Women*, June 29, 1995, no. 6 (published on the Internet by Catholic Resource Network, Trinity Communications). Also published by the United States Catholic Conference, Washington, D.C.

been based on a literal or fundamentalist interpretation of the Bible. The Bible is an important authority for Catholic theology, but scriptural verses and books are interpreted in relation to their own historical context, to complementary and mutually correcting themes within the Bible as a whole, to church traditions of theology and practice, and to contemporary needs and insights. Thus biblical references to "submission" and "headship" do not become red flags or litmus tests for Catholic identity in the way that they do in some Protestant denominations. (There is such a thing as "Catholic fundamentalism," but it is much more likely to focus on papal encyclicals and on Vatican decrees than on scriptural proof texts.)

The Common Good, the Person, and Women's Roles

In the one-hundred-year-old tradition of social encyclicals, the "common good" is a central concept. A representative statement comes from the 1963 encyclical of Pope John XXIII, *Peace on Earth*.[4] "Since men [and women] are social by nature they are meant to live with others and to work for one another's welfare."[5] Further, "the very nature of the common good requires that all members of the political community be entitled to share in it, although in different ways according to each one's tasks, merits and circumstances." "Justice and equity," however, can sometimes mandate that society and civil government "give more attention to the less fortunate members of the community, since they are less able to defend their rights and to assert their legitimate claims."[6] As long as thirty-five years ago, John XXIII realized that "women are taking a part in public life," "becoming ever more conscious of their human dignity," and thus "demand rights befitting a human person both in domestic and in public life."[7] John Paul II speaks more specifically of the equality of the sexes, similarly defending women's "rights and role within family and society."[8] He endorses "personal rights" and

4. John XXIII, *Peace on Earth*, in *Seven Great Encyclicals*, ed. William J. Gibbons, S.J. (Paulist: New York, 1963), pp. 289-335.
5. John XXIII, *Peace on Earth*, no. 31.
6. John XXIII, *Peace on Earth*, no. 56.
7. John XXIII, *Peace on Earth*, no. 41.
8. John Paul II, *On the Family*, no. 22.

"real equality in every area," including "equality of spouses with regard to family rights."[9]

Specifically on the family, the pope considers women's role as mother to have a special value, and even to manifest par excellence the "special genius of women."[10] Nonetheless, he does not limit women's place to the domestic sphere. Instead, he criticizes "a widespread social and cultural tradition" about "family life" that "has considered women's role to be exclusively that of wife and mother, without adequate access to public functions, which have generally been reserved for men." He insists, "There is no doubt that the equal dignity and responsibility of men and women fully justifies women's access to public functions." Proper education will guarantee that "discrimination between the different types of work and professions is eliminated at its very root," the "image of God in man and woman" being thereby illumined.[11] In his letter for Beijing, John Paul II expresses thanks not only to wives, mothers, and members of religious communities, but adds, "Thank you women who work! You are present and active in every area of life — social, economic, cultural, artistic and political."[12]

All this does not mean, however, that the pope sees women and men as identical in personality, gifts, or roles. Although women should have access to virtually all the social roles open to men, they will exercise these roles in different ways. John Paul II is a proponent of complementary gender characteristics, although not necessarily separate social roles. Clearly, this viewpoint helps retain a base in Catholic teaching for the exclusion of women from the ministerial priesthood.[13] Yet it also promotes respect for women who exercise the vocation of mother and remain in the home. The pope sees the parental roles of mother and father as cooperative and reciprocal, even suggesting that men "learn" fatherhood from women, whose experiences of pregnancy and birth enhance their predisposition "of paying attention to another person."[14] A feminist critique may fault the idea that women are in-

9. John Paul II, *Letter to Women*, no. 4.

10. John Paul II, *On the Dignity and Vocation of Women* (United States Catholic Conference: Washington, D.C., 1988), nos. 30-31; *Letter to Women*, nos. 9-11.

11. John Paul II, *On the Dignity and Vocation of Women*, no. 23.

12. John Paul II, *Letter to Women*, no. 2.

13. See, for example, John Paul II, *Letter to Women*, nos. 7, 11.

14. John Paul II, *Vocation of Women*, no. 18.

herently more sensitive to others than men, arguing that it consigns both sexes to constraining gender stereotypes and results ultimately in more passive and subordinate roles for women. Nevertheless, the pope explicitly rejects "a wrong superiority of male prerogatives which humiliates women and inhibits the development of healthy family relationships."[15]

Injustice Toward Women and the Christian Response

As a matter of historical fact, women have been subordinated to men, and this is a grave injustice. John Paul II, on behalf of the church and Christian tradition, even takes some responsibility for this situation. Women "have often been relegated to the margins of society and even reduced to servitude. . . . And if objective blame . . . has belonged to not just a few members of the church, for this I am truly sorry."[16] He mentions many examples, among them sexual violence, the prostitution of young girls, and the complicity of men and "the general social environment" in pressuring women into abortions.[17]

To formulate a Christian response, John Paul II adopts the special stance of support toward powerless groups that has uniformly marked his encyclical letters such as *The Gospel of Life*. In that letter he writes that Jesus of Nazareth "proclaims to all who feel threatened and hindered that their lives too are a good to which the Father's love gives meaning and value."[18] When it comes to setting women free from every kind of exploitation and domination, the gospel contains an ever-relevant message; transcending the established norms of his own culture, Jesus treated women with openness, respect, acceptance, and tenderness. In this way he honored the dignity which women have always possessed according to God's plan and in his love. As we look to Christ at this point in our history, it is natural to ask ourselves how much of his message has been heard and acted upon.[19]

The pope follows the tradition of modern Catholic social teach-

---

15. John Paul II, *On the Family,* no. 25.
16. John Paul II, *Letter to Women,* no. 3.
17. John Paul II, *Letter to Women,* no. 5.
18. John Paul II, *Gospel of Life* (Boston: Pauline, 1995), no. 32.
19. John Paul II, *Letter to Women,* no. 3.

ing by affirming a standard of justice as social equality and participation in the common good, then taking the Bible as an authority in establishing a special commitment to work for the "poor." This category includes all those who suffer unjust discrimination and exclusion for any reason. The example of Jesus is specifically used to show that women in general, though to a greater or lesser degree in varying cultural situations, belong in the category of those deserving affirmative, inclusive social support.

The Bible, the Family, and Gender Roles

It is clear that the pope regards subordination of women in the family to be an injustice, and therefore a violation of women's dignity and of the will of Christ. His approach is typically Catholic in that it does not rely on specific texts or sayings of Jesus taken out of context. Instead, it looks toward the integral example of Jesus and the basic orientation of the gospel.

It is in this spirit that John Paul II interprets particular biblical passages about the roles of women and men and about marriage and family. Two important examples are his treatment of Paul's letter to the Ephesians, chapter 5, where marriage is compared to the relation of Christ and church, and his discussion of the creation stories in Genesis, especially the story of the fall in chapter 3. The first of these two is the standard source of the concept of "headship," since in it Paul compares the love of husband for wife to that of Christ for the church, then adds that the husband is head of the wife just as Christ is head of the church. A full treatment of the controversies about interpretation of this text would go beyond the scope of this short essay of mine. Suffice it to say, for the purpose of explaining the contemporary Catholic view of the matter, that the pope devotes a full chapter of *Vocation of Women* to Ephesians' "bride and bridegroom" metaphor without ever bringing up the topic of "headship." The main point developed by the pope in this chapter is not the hierarchy of the sexes in marriage (an idea that is denied), but the permanent faithfulness of love in marriage, a faithfulness premised precisely on the mutuality and equality of the spouses.

In other words, the agenda is to affirm indissolubility, not hierarchy or headship. Indissolubility is an obligatory ideal for both women and men. Catholic teaching reinforces the bonds of married partners to their children by insisting on the close connection of sex and procreation. Having children is not the only purpose of sex, since sexual intimacy expresses and enhances the gift of self that constitutes marriage as a whole. But when sexual intimacy does result in pregnancy and birth, both partners bear important parental responsibilities in nurturing and educating their children. Men's loyalty to family ties need not and should not be purchased at the price of women's subordination to men's choices and demands. Both marriage and parenthood are the mutual, shared responsibilities of men and women.

On the pivotal text, "Wives, be subject to your husbands as you are to the Lord. For the husband is the head of the wife . . ." (Eph. 5:22-23), John Paul II differentiates the human love relation from that of Christ's to the church. He has already defined the comparison of husband to Christ as an analogy, not a literal statement. He now says that "whereas in the relationship between Christ and the Church the subjection is only on the part of the Church, in the relationship between husband and wife the 'subjection' is not one-sided but mutual." This mutuality, an attitude of generous love and self-gift, modeled for both wife and husband on the example of Christ, requires faithfulness from both partners. The recognition of the mutuality that properly characterizes marriage is dawning only gradually "in hearts, consciences, behavior and customs." Making equal, mutual, and faithful love a reality in marriage is a challenge in human history comparable, in the pope's view, to the abolition of slavery.[20]

Not relying on Ephesians alone, or even on the New Testament, to establish the relation of spouses in marriage, the pope also turns to the second Genesis creation story. Of particular interest in his reading are God's words addressed to the woman after the fall: "your desire shall be for your husband, and he shall rule over you" (3:16). In line with much recent feminist biblical interpretation, the pope concludes that this text outlines the consequences of sin, not God's will in creating the sexes. The image of God in both should be reflected in the "unity" of the woman and man; instead, "he shall rule over you" represents the threat of domination, a corruption of the good order of creation. "This 'domination' indicates the disturbance and loss of the stability of that

20. John Paul II, *Vocation of Women,* no. 24.

fundamental equality which the man and the woman possess in the 'unity of the two': and this is especially to the disadvantage of the woman. . . ." The relation of spouses intended by God, that which Christians must now aim to restore, is a "communion of persons," in which each gives "the gift of self" to the other.[21] The pope still maintains that women and men have different "masculine" and "feminine" personalities, but he does not interpret this complementarity as hierarchy, either in society or in marriage.

A question or problem created by the pope's definition of women and men as "different but equal" is whether the centrality that John Paul II attributes to motherhood in defining the feminine personality results in an imbalance in male and female roles, insofar as women are more responsible for children and less available for other social roles. Likewise, men's participation in the family is not equally encouraged and respected. This results in inequality, in that male and female spheres of activity are both limited in stereotypical ways. Moreover, "women's sphere" is socially less valued; and the preeminence of women even in the domestic realm is compromised by the economic dependence of most women and children "in the family" on men. These are all consequences that the pope wants to avoid. The dependency and inequality of women would be exacerbated still further if men were granted authority over women even in what is supposedly women's own particular and special sphere of competence; this is a move from which John Paul II distances himself. But the compatibility of complementarity and equality in defining gender roles needs further reflection and discussion.

Conclusions

The pope's general perspective on social ethics greatly influences his view of the institution of the family, and hence his approach to the relations of men and women in that institution. The pope understands every person as inherently social and does not portray families as "nuclear" units only, but as participating in and contributing to the common good by fulfilling many social roles. His perspective on families is

---

21. John Paul II, *Vocation of Women,* no. 10.

social and global, and, as always, he is very sensitive to economic patterns of injustice that exemplify domination of the weak by the strong. He is thus aware of the injustices to women that can distort family relations. Respect for the equality of women thus becomes part of the preferential option for the poor.

John Paul II is not unaware of threats to family life, including the danger that spouses will not honor their commitments to one another or to children. But the pope is essentially a "realistic idealist." He does not accept compromise with the harsh realities of life (like male infidelity) if he thinks that doing so will result in greater toleration of unfair human relationships. Although suffering is an unavoidable part of life, to be interpreted under the sign of the cross, the pope does not advise those who suffer to simply accept their lot. He is an untiring promoter of human rights and social reform and never ceases to appeal both to reason and to Christian faith in attempting to remedy injustice and transform evil situations. This applies to his approach to inequity between the sexes in the family and in society alike. An inegalitarian interpretation of certain Christian biblical texts cannot provide a charter for the treatment of women, since women's equality and dignity should be understood "from the use of reason itself," a use reflecting "the law of God written in the heart of every human being."[22] The equal dignity of women and men demands full and faithful mutuality in the family, not the subordination of one spouse to the other. The authentic norm of relations between the sexes in marriage is not hierarchy but "mutual self-gift."

22. John Paul II, *Letter to Women*, no. 7.

CHAPTER 6

**A Feminist Christian Theologian
Looks (Askance) at Headship**

Bonnie Miller-McLemore

ON THE DAY I had set aside to revise my remarks on male headship, I
arose to front-page headlines in *The Tennessean*, Nashville's main local
paper, that read, "[Southern] Baptists hone views on family," with the
subtitle, "Proposal bolsters heterosexual marriage."[1] The proposed
change for the "Baptist Faith and Message" statement — that marriage
is for heterosexuals only and wives should "submit graciously" to husbands — would not be received without challenge, however. The article
quoted a local Baptist minister who commented that the proposal disregarded the complex changes in gender roles, represented a poor attempt to go back to the hierarchical, male-dominated view of the family, and appeared to be one more effort to purge Baptist seminaries of
more progressive faculty. Of particular interest in the proposal was the
automatic link between upholding heterosexual marriage and asserting male headship. One wonders: can one support marriage without
endorsing male headship? As important, since male headship consistently receives biblical sanction as "God's Word," what do biblical texts
really say about male responsibilities within the household? Is male
headship a biblical absolute? Finally, I was once more reminded that
those with alternative views, among whom I would be numbered, have
our work cut out for us. If it took two centuries or more for this model
of family to become entrenched as an unquestioned household man-

1. *The Tennessean*, May 13, 1998, section 1, p. 1.

Parts of this paper appear in "Ideals and Realities of Motherhood: A Theological Perspective," in *Mother Troubles: Rethinking Contempory Maternal Dilemmas,* ed. Julia Hanigsberg and Sara Ruddick (Boston: Beacon, 1999), 281-303.

date, creating fresh Christian models of marriage grounded in shared responsibility and mutuality will require plenty of time, arduous work, and serious reflection as well.

Some Answers to Questions

> Yes, in a historical and descriptive sense, Christianity does teach male headship.

Without a doubt, Christianity has taught and continues to teach male headship. In fact, it is impossible to worship in the vast majority of Christian congregations across this country today, even in the more liberal churches, without endorsing male headship however subtly or indirectly. Ideals about gender roles are embedded in formative religious practices of men as elders and priests, in prayers, doxologies, and creeds praising a male deity, in the fact that women are relative newcomers to sacred rituals, and in the continued resistance to change in all of these areas. These practices have a hidden yet persuasive influence because they are embodied physically in word and in deed and repeated weekly in ritualized ceremonies of conviction and proclamation in settings that are unique in their cross-generational participation of children, youth, adults, and the elderly. For many people, worship is the primary encounter with particular religious ideals about gender and, at the very same time, the last place for critical reflection on these ideals. Ideals about the roles of the sexes and male headship are not only embedded in routine religious practices, they are intertwined with far-reaching historical and religious notions — Christian assumptions about suffering servanthood and self-sacrifice, Aristotelian and Christian codes defining the relationship between subordinate and superior family members, and other powerful motifs.

> No, in a normative sense, Christianity should not and the gospel does not teach male headship.

On the other hand, does the *gospel*, as distinct from *Christianity*, teach male headship? Should a Christianity true to its prophetic heritage teach male headship? These are different questions, to which many

Christian scholars would now respond with an emphatic "no." Indeed, the challenge to a religiously sanctioned male headship is not new. For at least the last two decades, feminist theologians have advocated the ideal of mutuality and shared responsibility in parenting and marriage as grounded in biblical, historical, contemporary, and practical studies in religion and theology.

Earlier this century, prominent Protestant theologians, such as Reinhold Niebuhr, saw mutuality as a relatively easy human achievement compared to the impossibility of realizing genuine *agape* or sacrificial love. Niebuhr portrayed selfless, unconditional love as the ideal and mutuality as only a necessary and limited compromise. In the last few decades, feminist theology has argued that this Protestant heritage has grossly oversimplified the significance of *caritas* and mutuality in Christian love. Radical mutuality is a transformative Christian ideal with potentially more dramatic consequences for families than sacrificial love.[2]

This is not to argue that equality, shared responsibility, and mutuality in marriage and parenting represent the Christian family any more than the nineteenth-century breadwinner/homemaker comprised the Christian family. I would argue, however, that in the current context "equal regard" is the most fitting ideal for Christian spouses and, furthermore, that it rests on rich resources in Christian Scripture and theology. As my co-authors and I claim in *From Culture Wars to Common Ground*,[3] one can detect trajectories in Christianity that point toward the egalitarian mother-father partnership. Moreover, our interviews, Gallup poll, and extensive study of the prominent voices in the family debate demonstrate that American society is undergoing a profound revolution in its image of marital and family love. But at the same time as many people perceive mutuality as essential to their lives, they struggle all the more to find the language to articulate it and the means to enact it.

2. Margaret Farley, "New Patterns of Relationship: Beginnings of a Moral Revolution," in *Woman: New Dimensions,* ed. Walter Burkhardt (New York: Paulist, 1976), pp. 51-70; Beverly Harrison, "The Power of Anger in the Work of Love: Christian Ethics for Women and Strangers," *Union Seminary Quarterly Review* 36 (1981): 41-57.

3. Don S. Browning, Bonnie J. Miller-McLemore, Pamela Couture, K. Brynolf Lyon, and Robert Franklin, *From Culture Wars to Common Ground: Religion and the American Family Debate* (Louisville: Westminster/John Knox, 1997).

In face of the gradual demise of the nineteenth-century ideal of sacrifice and headship and the current struggle to create new family models, *From Culture Wars to Common Ground* advances a new family ideal, what we call the committed equal-regard, public-private family.[4] Proponents of male headship insist that headship does not give license for domination; male headship, it is said, simply means that the husband has a special role in protecting, leading, edifying, and serving his wife and children. By contrast, however, the ideal of equal regard asserts that responsibility and leadership must be *shared*[5] and, furthermore, that this position has biblical warrant in creation and New Testament stories as well as practical benefits for couples, children, and the wider community. Family decisions require a process of equilateral conversation, a give and take uncharacteristic of the unilateral process of headship and submission in which ultimately one person — the husband and father — has final power over others.

Equal regard does not mean, however, that men and women do not have particular roles and unique contributions. "Equal" does not mean "same" or "identical." Women and men have distinctive contributions in bearing and rearing children, and children benefit from the contrast between parents. Parents adopt particular roles, but judgments about these roles remain open-ended, designed to honor physiological difference while not allowing it to dictate the specific behaviors, worth, or destiny of either parent. Most important, determinations about who is ultimately in charge are not made according to sex, nor is the distribution of privileges and responsibilities in both the public and private spheres of life decided by sex. Equal regard describes a relationship between husband and wife characterized by mutual respect, affection, practical assistance, and justice — a relationship that values and aids the self and others with equal seriousness. Among the advantages of such a relationship is that children raised within such a context benefit from the fuller participation of each parent in their lives and the living example of mutuality and justice between parents.

Granted, equal regard is a rigorous ethic, perhaps requiring

4. Browning et al., *From Culture Wars*, pp. 2-3. See also Bonnie J. Miller-McLemore, *Also a Mother: Work and Family As Theological Dilemma* (Nashville: Abingdon, 1994), and "Family and Work: Can Anyone Have It All?" in *Religion, Feminism, and the Family*, ed. Anne Carr and Mary Stewart Van Leeuwen (Louisville: Westminster/John Knox, 1996).
5. Browning et al., *From Culture Wars*, p. 245.

greater investment in straightforward dialogue about the needs, demands, desires, and hopes of family members and community. People often have to learn new patterns of communication. They endure the psychological dissonance of new roles and the social pressure to conform to dilapidated conventions and expectations, treading where their own parents have not trod. Moreover, establishing and maintaining the full equality between husband and wife requires an awareness and constant renegotiation of the often uneven distribution of private and public responsibilities and power between husband and wife. The unavoidable sacrifices requisite for sustaining family and work must be identified and shared, leaving commitment and mutuality, not duty and sacrifice, the central family motif.

Finally, it is important to note that one reason male headship survives is that implementing equal regard requires even wider society change. Shared responsibility between men and women in families cannot occur fully without an analogous restructuring of the ecology of supports for families so that extended family, church, civil society, government, and the market assist couples and children.

The question — Does Christianity teach male headship? — implies that the challenge to male headship is a new topic in Christian thought. The contradiction between this implication and the longevity of the discussion in feminist theology raises three questions worthy of further discussion: First, why has feminist theological discussion of this ideal been so overlooked in the family debate? Second, why are many people now able to talk about mutuality as preferable to headship but yet struggle to enact it? Finally, what are some of the contributions of Christian feminism?

Why has the Christian feminist voice been overlooked?

Feminist theology has been overlooked by secular feminists, social scientists, and policymakers alike — first, as a result of general public ignorance about the role of religion, and, second, as a result of the limited nature of most feminist theological approaches to families. Religion is one subject about which many feel free to claim expertise, and yet most are strikingly uninformed about the role of religion in public life and American history. Public dismissal of religion as a significant influence and as a field of study is unfortunate because it leaves an entire spectrum of human behavior and history unexplored.[6] This is even more troubling when limited views of "Christian" values, such as those of the Christian Coalition, are those automatically equated with the term. The media's tendency to portray religion in sound bites and in adversarial positions is partly responsible for such misperceptions. Nevertheless, public arguments for the values of justice, equal rights, responsibility, democracy, and so forth gain clarity, viability, and endurance from the study and practice of religion.

Second, feminist theological discussion of families has been limited. Few feminist theologians have entered into dialogue with secular feminist colleagues or wider publics. Moreover, feminist theology has focused its energies (for the most part justifiably so) on deconstructing the patriarchal family and its predilection toward violence and abuse. Only inadvertently and sporadically have feminist theologians attempted to offer new definitions of family ideals and practices. Feminist theologians have propounded the ideal of mutuality in various forms for the last three decades, but only a few have made efforts to modify it to fit the distinctiveness of family relationships.

A few feminist theologians apply to the parent-child relationship a prominent feminist theological interpretation of the "female problematic" — the proclivity of women, particularly mothers, toward self-dispersion, distractibility, and low esteem.[7] My own work as well as that of Christine Gudorf and Sally Purvis has asserted the dangers of self-fragmentation and the importance of self-fulfillment in the very act of giving to one's children, thereby further challenging traditional doctrines of sin as prideful self-assertion.[8] Gudorf recognizes the transitional sacrifices necessary for adequate mothering but holds mutual-

6. See Sara Ruddick, introduction to *Mother Troubles: Rethinking Contemporary Maternal Dilemmas*, ed. Julia Hanigsberg and Sara Ruddick (Boston: Beacon, 1999).

7. Valerie Saiving, "The Human Situation: A Feminine View," *Journal of Religion* (April 1960): 100-112; reprinted in Carol Christ and Judith Plaskow, eds., *Womanspirit Rising* (New York: Harper and Row, 1980), pp. 25-42.

8. See, for example, Miller-McLemore, *Also a Mother*, and "Family and Work"; Christine E. Gudorf, "Parenting, Mutual Love, and Sacrifice," in *Women's Consciousness and Women's Conscience: A Reader in Feminist Ethics,* ed. Barbara Hilkert Andolsen, Christine E. Gudorf, and Mary D. Pellauer (San Francisco: Harper and Row, 1985), and "Sacrifice and Parental Responsibilities," in *Religion, Feminism, and the Family,* pp. 294-309; Sally Purvis, "Mothers, Neighbors, and Strangers: Another Look at Agape," *Journal of Feminist Studies in Religion* 7, no. 1 (spring 1991): 19-34.

ity, rather than sacrifice, as the goal.[9] Here she argues for the relevance of Catholic ideas of charity that do not exclude the self in contrast to traditions shaped by the Protestant view that self-interest invalidates genuine Christian love (in Luther, Kierkegaard, Niebuhr, and Anders Nygren, for example). The meaning of Jesus' death itself assumes a different interpretation under this view. Less a sacrifice and more a consequence of the love for others, the cross calls people to renewed relations that may require moments of sacrifice but not to self-sacrifice as an end in and of itself. This may sound like a slight distinction but it makes all the difference in the world in people's lives. And this change in understanding is one of the hardest to implement in ritual practices since it requires changing the interpretation of the cross in powerful hymns or in communion liturgies at the center of most Christian worship.

Why is mutuality easier said than done?

I have already alluded to partial answers to my second question: Why the interest in mutuality but the unwillingness or inability to enact it? Does the routine use of language about egalitarian relationships simply cover over a host of subtle inequities between women and men in the particularities of their care for the home and children?

General public approval of equality and feminist theological discussion of mutuality have sometimes been sloppy. First, more often than not, the proclamation of mutuality and equality assumes a relationship between two relatively equal adults. The difficult questions arise, however, when one strives to maintain the ideal of mutuality in *nonequal* relationships, and in the practice of parenting, equal relationships are rare. Besides the differences between parent and child — in particular the greater authority and responsibility borne by the parent for the life of the child — the affirmation of mutuality and equality has also assumed sameness between mothers and fathers, who are in fact different in relation to their children. Proponents of mutuality must take into account the divergent developmental demands of parent and child in raising children. These demands fluctuate as children grow, demanding special responses from each parent, including responses

9. Gudorf, "Parenting, Mutual Love, and Sacrifice," pp. 182, 186.

particular to a spouse's sexual identity. Just as the parents reach some semblance of just balance in the participation of each parent in response to the needs of the child and the home, the child grows and the needs change, especially during the early years of a child's life. The elementary and adolescent years also require certain sex-specific parental responses. This still does not preclude the ideal of radical mutuality between parents; it does require, however, that its boundaries be renegotiated yet again. Unfortunately, few discussions of mutuality as an ideal have taken these kinds of developmental realities and family negotiations into consideration.

Second, with the free and easy use of the term "mutuality" these days, the concrete demands of domestic life often drop out of the equation. The movement from "rhetoric to reality" in practical equality between women and men[10] has to reckon with factors as diverse as the inefficiency of shared responsibility when rotating domestic chores prevents either spouse from acquiring expediency (e.g., in grocery shopping or laundry), the limited time in a day for parents who assume multiple roles, the pressures of the biology and psychology of childbearing toward inequity, the powerful force of socialization toward male headship, the economic disparity between men and women and between races and classes, the materialistic pressures of a capitalistic market economy and the reduction of leisure time, and the economic demands for geographic mobility that sometimes require incomparable sacrifices of one partner.

Both of these oversights — the assumption of sameness in conceptions of mutuality and the overlooking of the complexity of domestic life — lead to the neglect of the tricky question of how and where certain sacrifices and certain kinds of leadership or authority become requisite as a means to maintain mutuality and equality, for certainly sacrifice and authority still have their place. They have their place both in the unequal relationship between parents and children and in the midst of the practical demands of the equal relationship between mothers and fathers. The challenge is parceling out leadership, respon-

---

10. Herbert Anderson, "Between Rhetoric and Reality: Women and Men as Equal Partners in Home, Church, and the Marketplace," *Word and World: Theology for Christian Ministry* 17, no. 4 (fall 1997): 376-86. See also Pauline Kleingeld, "Just Love? Marriage and the Question of Justice," *Social Theory and Practice* 24, no. 2 (1998).

sibilities, and sacrifices over the long haul of family evolution while keeping an eye on the prize of achieving new family ideals of equal regard and mutuality.

What are some of Christian feminism's contributions?

Ignorance about feminist theological scholarship is unfortunate because several themes in feminist theology offer avenues through the impasses in the secular debate over the family. I will highlight four. First, from early on Christian feminists have contested the idealization of female self-sacrifice,[11] and more recently womanist theologians have questioned ideals of suffering servanthood and female subordination in religious practice.[12] My mention of Gudorf's and my own work thus depicts only the crest of a wave of far more extensive thematic discussion by several other theologians (male and female) of the problems with sacrificial models of love for women and of the importance of redefining love in terms of *caritas*.

Second, feminist theologians generally repudiate two conventional dualisms. They resist falling on either side of the polarized conflict between those who interpret the current family disruption as a decline caused by individualism and other values of modern culture, and those who interpret the disruption as being caused by the destructive economic values of materialistic capitalism. And of more relevance to the topic of headship, feminist theologians walk the fine line between those who portray gender as a strictly natural, biological reality (arguing, for example, that women are instinctively more nurturing than men) and those who believe that human sexuality (and the so-called instinct for nurture) are completely social constructions based on particular relative cultural expectations. Almost all feminists in both Jewish

11. See, for example, Saiving, "The Human Situation,"; Farley, "New Patterns of Relationship"; Judith Plaskow, *Sex, Sin, and Grace: Women's Experience and the Theologies of Reinhold Niebuhr and Paul Tillich* (Washington, D.C.: University Press of America, 1980); Barbara Hilkert Andolsen, "Agape in Feminist Ethics," *Journal of Religious Ethics* 9 (spring 1981): 69-83; Harrison, "Power of Anger."

12. See Jacquelyn Grant, "The Sin of Servanthood and the Deliverance of Discipleship," and Frances E. Wood, "'Take My Yoke Upon You': The Role of the Church in the Oppression of African-American Woman," both in *A Troubling in My Soul: Womanist Perspectives on Evil and Suffering*, ed. Emilie M. Towns (Maryknoll, N.Y.: Orbis, 1993).

and Christian traditions share a holistic or anti-dualistic understanding of flesh and spirit as inseparable. Gender roles then are neither a mechanical reflex of biology nor solely a social construction with no biological referents. Gender roles in childbirth and even child-rearing are to some extent "bio-social" events; roles and duties in parenting are social and physical arrangements women and men must constantly renegotiate in face of both natural circumstance and historical, social contingency. Gender stereotypes signal an onerous breakdown in this process with negative consequences for all involved.

Third, feminist theology also suggests that a feminist social agenda is not well served by the neglect of the institutional dimensions of families. A crucial distinction between motherhood as experience and motherhood as institution was introduced in 1976 by Adrienne Rich in her book *Of Woman Born*. In her words, the institution is superimposed on the experience and aims at ensuring that the "*potential relationship* of any woman to her powers of reproduction and to children . . . remain under male control."[13] The institution of motherhood under patriarchy thwarts women's freedom, alienates them from their bodies, and corrupts fatherhood, all through three generic precepts: "all women are seen primarily as mothers; all mothers are expected to experience motherhood unambivalently and in accordance with patriarchal values; and the 'nonmothering' woman is seen as deviant."[14] Yet, as Rich establishes so well, all mothers feel ambivalent and some women chose not to mother for good reasons. Through the courage and intensity of her prose, readers encounter the mother as a person with needs, desires, and thoughts of her own. In part as a result of Rich's work, some of the patriarchal dimensions of the institution have less hold than they once did.

The ensuing years have shown, however, that the relationship between the institution and the experience of motherhood is more complex than Rich assumes. The distinction of experience and institution has proved helpful in seeing the fuller reality of women's lives, but ultimately the contrast is not between, on the one hand, patriarchal institutions and a patriarchal society and, on the other, maternal experience and nature

---

13. Adrienne Rich, *Of Woman Born: Motherhood As Experience and Institution* (New York: W. W. Norton, 1976), p. 13.

14. Adrienne Rich, "Motherhood in Bondage (1976)," in *On Lies, Secrets, and Silence: Selected Prose 1966-1978* (New York: W. W. Norton, 1979), pp. 195-97.

but, as Judith Plaskow argues, "between oppressive institutions and institutions that are life-enhancing."[15] Respecting the experiences of mothers requires creating and maintaining social institutions of family, marriage, partnership, and motherhood that secure the good of mothers and the good of others. In other words, Jewish and Christian feminists generally have not found either the rejection of women's bodily experience in patriarchy or the exaltation of it in radical feminist theory a sufficient option. In part, this is because feminist theologians grapple with complex historical images of women's experience, the valuable, albeit ambiguous, contributions of social institutions, and religious traditions in which intricate human relationship is mediated through the flesh.

Finally — and this point is perhaps the most relevant for this discussion — Christian feminism has effectively established radical mutuality as more than a humanitarian interest. Mutuality has ontological or divine warrant in a Trinitarian, relational godhead where God is understood as three-persons-in-one and in need of human relationship.[16] In other words, fresh interpretations of the Trinity lift up the idea of a complex relationality at the center of the divine rather than an omnipotent, all powerful, but basically independent supreme being. Mutuality also has biblical warrant in the early Christian communities.[17] Despite the patriarchal character of the ancient societies in which Christianity arose and despite the ways in which the Christian tradition has perpetuated ideals of male dominance in the centuries since, such patriarchy is not the last word; scholars such as Elisabeth Schüssler Fiorenza claim that in Mark's Gospel, for example, women emerge as the "true Christian ministers and witnesses" and the most courageous of all Christ's disciples.[18]

15. Plaskow, *Sex, Sin, and Grace*, p. 57.

16. Elizabeth A. Johnson, *She Who Is: The Mystery of God in Feminist Theological Discourse* (New York: Crossroad, 1992); Catherine La Cugna, *God for Us: The Trinity and Christian Life* (New York: Harper, 1991).

17. Rosemary Radford Ruether, *Sexism and God-Talk: Toward a Feminist Theology* (Boston: Beacon, 1983), and "An Unrealized Revolution: Searching Scripture for a Model of the Family," *Christianity and Crisis* (Oct. 31, 1983), pp. 399-404; see also Ruether's "Church and Family I: Church and Family in the Scriptures and Early Christianity," *New Blackfriars* (Jan. 1984), pp. 4-14.

18. Elisabeth Schüssler Fiorenza, "In Search of Women's Heritage," in *Weaving the Visions: New Patterns in Feminist Spirituality*, ed. Judith Plaskow and Carol P. Christ (New York: Harper and Row, 1989), p. 31; see also her *In Memory of Her: A Feminist Theological Reconstruction of Christian Origins* (New York: Crossroad, 1984).

Others confirm the relatively prominent role of women in early Christianity.[19] Still others explain the contradiction between Paul's insistence on the silence of women in the church in 1 Corinthians 14:34-35 and the inclusivity of his message elsewhere as a concession to the prevailing values of his time or even as the imposition and addition of someone else's words. In other words, over against social convention certain kinds of egalitarian premises characterized the early Christian movement. I am not arguing, of course, that the general public must believe and abide by these particular Christian faith tenets to realize good parenting or vital marriages. I simply observe that to the extent that religious ideals shape families and culture and to the extent that Christians choose to ground their ideas about gender roles in theology and Scripture, then ample grounds exist within Christianity for ideals other than male headship.

Perhaps the hardest texts to contend with and the texts that have most influenced the ideal of male headship are the household codes of the New Testament. "Household codes" is a term applied to scriptural passages that sought to order family relationships among early Christian converts in two deutero-Pauline letters (letters attributed to but not authored by Paul) of the New Testament, Colossians and Ephesians.[20] Typically in the household codes and similar passages, family members are exhorted to certain behaviors in relation to one another, particularly subordinates (e.g., wives, slaves, children) to their superiors (e.g., husbands, masters, fathers). These texts are particularly problematic for feminist interpretations of mutuality.[21] Regardless of their initial intention or interpretation, from at least the Reformation to the last century they have given supernatural sanction to patriarchal family roles in which men lead and women follow. More recently, the

19. See, for example, Virginia Ramey Mollenkott, *Women, Men, and the Bible* (Nashville: Abingdon, 1977); Elisabeth M. Tetlow, *Women and Ministry in the New Testament* (New York: Paulist, 1980); Ben Witherington, *Women in the Ministry of Jesus* (New York: Cambridge University Press, 1984).

20. The term also sometimes alludes to similar or related codes in 1 Timothy, Titus, and 1 Peter, although these passages are less tightly structured and are related to broader guidelines for congregations and communities.

21. See also, on gender, race, and the codes, Clarice J. Martin, "The Haustafeln (Household Codes) in African American Biblical Interpretation: 'Free Slaves' and 'Subordinate Women'," in *Story the Road We Trod: African American Biblical Interpretation*, ed. Cain Hope Felder (Minneapolis: Fortress, 1991), pp. 206-31.

household codes echo in the background of the handbook for the Promise Keepers' movement. Similarly, points 2, 3, and 6 of the "Danvers Statement" issued by the Council on Biblical Manhood and Womanhood (which was formed in 1989) declare gender roles to be ordained by God and redemption as consisting in loving leadership by husbands and willing submission by wives.

There are sufficient grounds for arguing, however, that the codes were not intended to bolster but to reverse ancient heroic models of male authority in families. In the household codes in Ephesians, for example, the author borrows and yet transmutes the metaphors of the surrounding male culture of strength, dominance, and conflict to suggest new virtues of peace, humility, patience, and gentleness. The husband is called to the self-giving love of Christ and to a kind of mutual subjection not found in similar Aristotelian codes. The code in Ephesians balances compliance with the patriarchal social mores of the times with ideas about submission and reciprocity in the Christian proclamation.[22] The very need for household codes in the deutero-Pauline letters may itself testify to the disruptive reality of a new family ethic evolving in the early Christian house church movement.[23]

Over history, it is this accent on male subordination that has been most overlooked. Instead women, more than men, have tended to absorb the message of sacrifice and submission. On occasion, when men have heard the Christian message, they have become less dominant and more giving. Nonetheless, as advocates of women, religious feminists often deride the codes as a reversal of the more inclusive message within the early Christian community, a reversal caused by the social and political pressures of the patriarchal society of that time. Particularly for women and children who have suffered domestic violence or physical or sexual abuse within Christian contexts upholding male authority, soft patriarchy is simply too high a price to pay for maintaining "stable" family life. Although the biblical passages themselves do not fully articulate new roles for women, reaching only a modified or benevolent patriarchy, it is nevertheless clear that the hierarchical pat-

22. Frank Stagg, "The Gospel, Haustafel, and Women: Mark 1:1; Colossians 3:18–4:1," *Faith and Mission* 2, no. 2 (1985).

23. See David Balch, *Let Wives Be Submissive: The Domestic Code in 1 Peter* (Atlanta: Scholars Press, 1981).

terns of the Greco-Roman world were, if not completely challenged, at least mitigated in the household codes as well as in some important aspects of the Jesus movement and in some of the practices of the early church.

While Christianity cannot provide comprehensive answers to the complex quandaries about gender roles and male dominance, one can hardly challenge male headship without confronting powerful religious representations and worldviews. In this context, recent reflection among feminists in religion suggests that fresh ideals for families will emerge from reinterpreted Christian understandings.

PART II **ITS CRITICS**

CHAPTER 7

The Problem of Men, Reconsidered

John W. Miller

DON BROWNING'S search for common ground in the culture wars of our time has landed him in a battle zone between those calling for gender equality and those calling for responsible male headship. His espousal of a marital ethic of equal regard resonates with feminist concerns about inequality between the sexes and male abuse of power. But he has also identified a looming "world fatherhood problem" that draws him toward those espousing male headship. At its center is what he terms a "male problematic" (defined as "male ambivalence toward fatherhood") which must also be addressed if the drift toward father absence and neglect in our culture is to be abated. To harmonize these dissimilar interests, insights, and goals, Browning seeks to weave his thinking about the male problematic and how to confront it into his proposed marital ethic of equal regard. In the process he runs the risk of weakening and losing touch with his own best insights into the marital crisis of our time and what can be done about it.

Disconnect between Equal Regard and the Male Problematic

At the beginning of his essay in this book, Browning is unequivocal in his advocacy of equal regard as the normative Christian teaching and is thus sharply critical of those who on the basis of New Testament teachings advocate the strengthening of marriages by calling upon men to take headship roles in their families. They should realize, he writes, that these teachings are a reflection of the patriarchal Greco-Roman honor-shame culture in which Christianity initially spread. Yet, midway through his essay, as he considers the male problematic, he acknowledges that "more" is needed than an ethic of equal regard. Indeed, the "more" that is needed, he explains, is precisely the New Testament teaching on male servant headship. Browning is aware of the disconnect and so refers again, at the close of his essay, to those he had earlier criticized for promoting teachings of male headship. Now, however, he applauds them for being "more aware of the male problematic" than their liberal counterparts.

His only remaining criticism is that these groups (Protestant evangelicals, the African-American church, the Roman Catholic Church) "are wrong in believing that male responsibility must necessarily be coupled with models of male headship." It would be better, he implies, if the ideal of "male servant headship" would be redefined as "servanthood," located "as a moment . . . within love as mutuality," and then applied equally to husbands and wives. But is this redefined teaching what wives actually need if "male ambivalence to fatherhood" is to be addressed? Can such a generalized and degenderized teaching still speak to the male problematic? Browning is aware of the problem. He acknowledges the inadequacies of a marital ethic of equal regard for dealing with the male problematic and concedes that New Testament headship teaching does effectively address this issue. *What he does not show is how this New Testament teaching remains effective when stripped of its specificity for men and redefined as he proposes.*

This dilemma is highlighted by what Browning himself has written elsewhere about the impotence of an ethic of equal regard in the face of the male problematic in today's culture. What we face today, he has said, is not so much male domination as male "neglect, absence and failure of responsibility." In the same essay he writes: "Modern men seem increasingly unable to live by an ethic of equal regard which renounces control but maintains high degrees of mutual respect with spouses and paternal investment in children."[1] If this is so, how germane is an ethic of equal regard? It would seem that a prior and far

---

1. Don Browning, "Biology, Ethics, and Narrative in Christian Family Theory," in *Promises to Keep: Decline and Renewal of Marriage in America,* ed. David Popenoe, Jean Bethke Elshtain, and David Blankenhorn (Lanham, Md.: Rowan and Littlefield, 1996), p. 142.

greater need is an ethic of fatherhood specifying what is required of men and women to create families where males are present in mutually loving relationships with their spouses and children — for how can males express love as equal regard in their marriages and families if in growing numbers they abandon or neglect their families?

I do not see either Browning or his colleagues, in the series of books they have published, squarely facing up to the contradictions that arise when the need to address the male problematic is subordinated to an ethic of equal regard.[2] Indeed, the major thrust of these volumes is subversive of the values of male headship — the very values that Browning rightly identifies as crucial for addressing the male problematic. For Browning's colleagues, however, these values are viewed as a legacy of male-dominated patriarchal culture that must be abandoned in favor of gender equality. Among these authors, Browning is unique in his identification of the male problematic as an issue of critical importance. But even his analysis is blunted, and at times lost, due to his desire to force-fit these insights into the larger framework of equal regard.

What is urgently needed right now in North America is a discussion of the male problematic in and of itself, especially as it relates to family breakdown. As Theodore Stoneberg puts it, "The overarching task for the twenty-first century is to reconnect manhood and fatherhood in the lives of Western men."[3] Browning's insights in this regard might well serve as the catalyst for such a discussion.

---

2. Browning confuses matters even further with his identification of a "female problematic," which he characterizes as an "easier commitment to the child but more ambiguous commitment to the husband" ("Biology, Ethics, and Narrative," p. 148), and with his subsequent discussion of love as equal regard being available for tempering both it and the male problematic, "as different as they are" (p. 150). How different are they? By his own definition the male and female problematic converge on the same issue: ambivalence toward fatherhood (males being ambivalent about becoming fathers to their own children; females being ambivalent about including males as fathers of their children). Hence the female problematic intensifies the impediments to fatherhood posed by the male problematic, making it even more important that this issue be addressed in its own right, and not buried within an ethic of equal regard.

3. Theodore Stoneberg, "The Tasks of Men in Families," in *The Family Handbook*, ed. Herbert Anderson, Don Browning, Ian S. Evison, and Mary Stewart Van Leeuwen (Louisville: Westminster/John Knox, 1998), p. 71.

Christianity and Greco-Roman Patriarchy

Browning has much to say about Christianity and Greco-Roman patriarchy. His thoughts seem initially in accord with the perspectives of his colleagues, namely, that the male honor-shame values of this culture are regrettable, as is the degree to which Christianity compromised itself by incorporating its model of male headship. But almost immediately, as he considers the male problematic, Browning's thoughts move in another direction. It would be wrong, he now explains, to think of Christianity as simply capitulating to Greco-Roman patriarchal culture, for there are marked contrasts between the *kind* of male headship promoted in Christian teachings and the kind idealized in Greco-Roman culture. Comparing the two, he concludes that although "primitive Christianity never completely escaped the honor-shame codes of Roman Hellenism, it did fracture or partially undermine them" and it was moving "away from" them.

The terms "fracture," "undermine" and move "away from" are confusing and invalid in light of what Browning subsequently writes about these two codes. At the heart of the Greco-Roman code were males who, though promiscuous themselves, were so protective of the sexual fidelity of the women in their own households that they felt honor bound to retaliate against sexual predators. Browning notes that Christianity was also concerned about sexual fidelity in marriage, so much so that fidelity was required of both wives *and* husbands. In addition, Christian men were encouraged to love their wives with the self-giving love exemplified in Jesus Christ (Eph. 5:25). So what then was "fractured"? Certainly not the core value of sexual fidelity between wives and their husbands, the sine qua non for paternal certainty and investment, nor the importance of the father-involved household. The only thing that was "fractured" (and not only fractured) was the male's right to treat his wife differently than he would want to be treated (equal regard), and, perhaps, the need to retaliate against sexual predators for the sake of male honor.

Biblical codes did not undermine, subvert, or destroy their patriarchal counterparts in the wider culture. They modified them, a point Browning himself makes in another essay. Relying on concepts drawn from evolutionary ecology, Browning describes the Greco-Roman honor-shame code as "a particular cultural elaboration of ancient male reproductive strategies; it was a way of controlling wives, assuring paternal certainty, but also exploring the advantages of the R-strategy [permission for limited male promiscuity]." Christianity, he then suggests, was exploring still another strategy.[4] Although he does not spell this out, its ethic too might be characterized as a way of "assuring paternal certainty" and "exploring the advantages" of the K-strategy (proscription of male promiscuity).[5] It is therefore misleading when Browning states that Christianity "fractured" Greco-Roman patriarchy and was "moving away" from it. Rather, by curtailing male promiscuity and establishing males in caring husband/father roles in families, it was addressing precisely the same issues in modified ways.

The Origins and Consequences of the Male Problematic

Don Browning is unique among Christian ethicists in the degree to which he draws upon the insights of evolutionary biology for an understanding of contemporary family issues and for developing a marital ethic that might guide us today. But additional work is needed in this area — the male problematic (ambivalence about fatherhood) might be more serious than Browning's analysis suggests.[6]

For example, in his essay in this volume, Browning seeks an understanding of this problematic by examining it in the context of the history of the species. He notes that "male primates, for the most part, do not help care for their infants after fathering them." Then, drawing on insights from evolutionary psychology and Thomas Aquinas, he advances four "natural factors" that influenced human males to become involved in families with their own children. First, due to the long period of infant dependency, females solicited male help in raising their offspring. Second, the male eventually came to recognize that a particular child was his and hence an extension of his own biological exis-

---

4. Browning, "Biology, Ethics, and Narrative," p. 142.

5. Regarding these terms taken from evolutionary theorists, see Browning, "Biology, Ethics, and Narrative," p. 123. The K-strategy invests a large set of resources into raising only a few children to adulthood; the R-strategy procreates a large number of offspring (the case of fish and frogs), leaving it to chance as to whether a few survive.

6. Further to my own views on this, see John W. Miller, *Biblical Faith and Fathering: Why We Call God 'Father'"* (New York: Paulist, 1989), chaps. 2 and 3.

tence. Third, sexual exchange further integrated the male into a more stable relation with his female partner. And finally, mutual assistance between male and female further consolidated their relationship.

These four items need to be carefully assessed and assembled into a credible storyline for how the two-parent, father-involved family might have actually emerged historically. Browning focuses on item two of this list, the recognition of the male that a specific child is his. Browning believes that this stage in the evolution of the family was facilitated by what evolutionary psychologists term "kin altruism" — that is, "that all creatures, including humans, are more likely to invest in and sacrifice for those who share their own genes than they are for nonkin." In Browning's view this was and is a "major . . . factor behind paternal recognition and investment." For him this means that the Christian virtues of love and self-sacrifice do not operate in a vacuum, but "build on and guide natural kin altruism." If kin altruism is the "natural" force in paternal recognition and investment Browning intimates it is, perhaps we can be a little less anxious about the fate of "fatherless America." Apparently there are powerful, natural forces at work predisposing males toward caring for their offspring.

But is this the case? In weighing the role of "paternal kin altruism" in family formation, it is very important that a clear distinction be made between "recognition" and "investment." Kin altruism plays no role at all in *paternal* "recognition."[7] Paternal recognition is a far more complex and difficult stage in the emergence of the father-involved family than is generally realized. For a given male to recognize that a given child is his requires, first of all, that the males and females in a given culture are aware of the part played by male insemination in the procreation of children. For this awareness to exist, a prior discovery must be made that this in fact is the case and this knowledge must be disseminated and appropriated. Bronislaw Malinowsky's research among certain primitive Melanesian tribes who did not have this

---

7. In an earlier essay, "Biology, Ethics, and Narrative," p. 123, Browning notes that paternal certainty is a key step in the emergence of paternal investment, but he seems to lose sight of this distinction in his essay here. I note a similar confusion in the discussion of these issues in David Popenoe, *Life without Father* (New York: Free Press, 1996). Popenoe argues strongly at times for a biological predisposition in males for paternity (p. 170) but then also recognizes loss of "paternity confidence" as a powerful factor in "today's downward spiral of fatherhood" (p. 175).

knowledge or awareness, and thought women became pregnant through departed spirits, affords a graphic illustration of what human cultures were like prior to this discovery. These tribes had no word for "father" since as far as they knew that relationship did not exist. Consequently, "between the father and the children there is no union whatsoever," Malinowsky reports. Instead, the children living with a certain mother regarded her male companion as "stranger" or "outsider."[8] Children were regarded instead as belonging exclusively to the mother and her extended family, and in point of fact came into the custody of the mother's brother as they grew older. Thus, in this phase of cultural development *paternal* kin altruism (in the sense of a male recognizing certain children as his and assuming responsibility for them) played no role whatsoever.

Only when the male knows that a given child is his through an act of insemination does kin altruism even begin to become a factor in the male's "investment" in his own children. But how great a factor is it even then? And what role does it actually play in two-parent family formation? In thinking this through it must be remembered that *maternal* kin altruism has always been a powerful force in the life of women. Among Malinowsky's Melanesian Trobrianders, the children born to the mother were regarded as belonging to her and her family. Thus, when considering the role of this "force of nature" in family formation, the unbalanced and competing ways it manifests itself in the experiences of males and females must be kept in mind. Also important are the contexts and circumstances in which paternal recognition occurs, whether in the matrix of a meaningful marriage, or as the consequence of a brief and casual sexual affair, or even as the consequence of rape.

Our current experience in North America, as sexual restraints erode and marriage is deinstitutionalized, replicates the experience of human cultures throughout history. Males are generally less tied by kin altruism to the children they sire than are women to the children born of their bodies. As a consequence, the number of single-parent families headed by mothers has grown alarmingly and far exceeds those headed by single-parent fathers. To cite just one statistic: in the United States

8. Bronislaw Malinowski, *The Father in Primitive Psychology* (New York: W. W. Norton, 1927), p. 12.

in 1995, nineteen million children lived with only one parent; of these children 87 percent lived with their mother.[9]

Human societies have learned that paternal kin altruism can and generally will become a "natural force" only when males are securely established in families and given a recognized and respected role as fathers of their own children. For this to happen, a monogamous companionate-sexual bond is far more important than kin altruism. Because human sexual pair bonds are fragile, however, they need strong cultural affirmation and support. As David Popenoe writes,

> Because men are only weakly attached to the father role and because men's reproductive and parental strategies are variable, culture is central to enforcing high paternal investment. In every society the main cultural institution designed for this purpose is marriage. Father involvement with children is closely linked to the quality of the relationship between husband and wife.[10]

Consider also an important point by Peter Wilson:

> An adult female will be naturally transformed into a social mother when she bears a child, but there is no corresponding natural transformation for a male. If he becomes a social father he does so only culturally or symbolically and, as it were, by permission of the female. . . . Only if we bear in mind this meaning of "father" and the vulnerability of the father to nature and the female can we explain the dominance of the male/father in all human cultures, which can first be seen in the asymmetry between the relations of mother/offspring and father/offspring.[11]

Here, then, is the urgent issue now facing us: Where can we turn for the cultural energy now needed to affirm and support families marked by "high paternal investment"? I do not believe that Browning is able to show that we will accomplish this through an androgynous ethic of equal regard that obscures the gender-specific cultural chal-

9. Cited from U.S. congressional documents in Wade F. Horn, *Father Facts,* 3d ed. (The National Fatherhood Initiative, 1998), p. 12.

10. Popenoe, *Life without Father,* p. 184.

11. Peter Wilson, *Man, the Promising Primate: The Conditions of Human Evolution,* 2d ed. (New Haven: Yale University Press, 1983), p. 71.

lenges involved in males becoming responsible fathers. I see no other way for fatherhood to emerge as the distinctive characteristic of a given society than for human thought to be ignited by a spark of wisdom that *clearly* discerns — and passionately so — that for human well-being and happiness the two-parent father-involved family is an essential institution. When this happens — whether through the voices of prophets or lawmakers or social scientists or teachers, or as a groundswell of conviction — guidelines, symbols, words, and rituals will be put in place restricting sexual promiscuity, honoring motherhood *and* fatherhood, and encouraging the formation of homes in which a certain woman will agree to live in sexual fidelity with a certain man who will covenant to be faithful to her, love her, protect her, and share in the care of the children born to them.

CHAPTER 8

The Problem of Protestants

Allan C. Carlson

CAN A "critical familism" informed by modern feminism, resting on "a full equality between husband and wife," and building on "an analysis of the power relations between husband, wife, children, and surrounding institutions," be reconciled with vital Christianity? A team of authors, led by Don S. Browning, take on the task of doing so in the volume *From Culture Wars to Common Ground: Religion and the American Family Debate.*[1]

On one level, their purpose is laudable. They seek to move beyond the "culture wars" over the family that have marked, and polarized, American political life in recent years. They seek to understand and encourage a "new family revolution," one freed from the errors of the past, and one suitable to the "religiocultural revolution in our time." In confronting the modern "male" and "female problematic," both of which involve a retreat from marriage, they long for stronger homes, fewer divorces, and happier children. In doing so, they seek to move beyond the language of male "headship" and female "submission" in marriage, arguing that such terms no longer bear cultural relevance. And they believe that an ethic of "equal regard" can accomplish all of these goals.

On another level, however, there is in their work a tendency to want the unattainable. They seek a family ethos that will transform lives, but also one that is "less pious in tone" and less under the sway of "confessing churches." They want a familism informed by the modern

---

1. Co-authors are Bonnie J. Miller-McLemore, Pamela D. Couture, K. Brynolf Lyon, and Robert M. Franklin (Louisville: Westminster/John Knox, 1997).

sciences, one "more interdisciplinary and interprofessional," but yet one also "more at the grassroots level." These apparent contradictions — a life-changing philosophy separated from vigorous faith and a professionally oriented ethos that is popular among the masses — point to deeper problems in their analysis.

Some Problems

Problem One

To begin with, in seeking to build a scriptural case for the concept of "equal regard," the authors have wandered into a new version of what might be called "the Protestant problematic." Specifically, they choose to lift and emphasize some parts of the New Testament out of the context of the whole; and they move close to embracing their own canon. On pages 146-47, for example, the authors state,

> This failure [of the author of Ephesians] to return and tell the second half of the story indicates the extent to which the epistle still reflected the andro-centrism of the ancient world. . . . [T]he letter to the Ephesians provocatively but incompletely challenges male authority in families. Our complaint should be that it did not complete its trajectory.

Also on page 147, they discuss "the post-Pauline conservative retreat" from an imputed early Christian experimentation with gender egalitarianism, back toward Aristotelian household codes premised on honor and shame. This supposed retreat can be seen, they say, in 1 and 2 Timothy, Titus, and 1 Peter, the New Testament books that an "equal regard" Lutheran would label as the new "epistles of straw." And on page 284, the authors add: "[I]f Ephesians has validity for today, it must be interpreted reversibly in all respects — as applying to the wife as profoundly as it does the husband." Presumably, if not so interpreted, Ephesians should then be dropped as invalid.

One suspects that the volume collides here indirectly with the problem openly stated by theologian Rosemary Radford Reuther: "Feminist theology cannot be done from the existing base of the Christian Bible." Instead, "a new Canon" would have to be created to square the circle.[2]

The obvious critical response is that the Epistle of Ephesians did not "complete its trajectory" because it was not intended to. Similarly, the Pastoral Epistles describe relations between men and women so as to protect biblical — or now "Christian" — forms of behavior from false teachers. If one acknowledges the divine inspiration of the biblical canon, this means that the message of Mark and Acts is to be understood in light of Ephesians and the Pastoral Epistles, and viceversa. (Of course, if one can choose one's own canon, all things are possible.)

Problem Two

What is more problematic, the argument of *From Culture Wars to Common Ground* presumes a fairly rigid ideological grid, running from patriarchy on the right to egalitarian feminism on the left, as in:

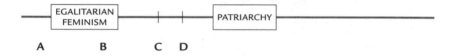

Here, the Old Testament social code might be represented by "C" and the Greco-Roman "honor-shame codes" by "D," while the early "Jesus Movement" is at "A" and the "post Pauline/Pastoral Epistles" church rests at "B." The task, then, would be to use the theology of "equal regard" to move Christianity leftward from "B" to "A."

Yet this kind of thinking fundamentally distorts the true beauty and revolutionary qualities of Christian marriage. While it might be true to say that the "patriarchal structure remains intact" in the post-Pauline Christian community, it has been radically altered, indeed turned upside down, to refocus on the wife's well-being (Eph. 5:23-28). In holding headship, the husband is charged with self-renouncing sac-

2. Rosemary Radford Reuther, *Womanguides: Readings Toward a Feminst Theology* (Boston: Beacon, 1985), p. ix.

rifice, while the wife's submission is directed toward the reconciliation of all things, including their marriage, to God.[3]

Indeed, the Ephesians text gives a christological foundation to male headship in Christian marriage. Headship is not a mere accommodation to human weakness, or to pressures of the surrounding pagan culture. Rather, Paul directly bonds male authority and responsibility to the model of Christ: "For the husband is the head of the wife just as Christ is the head of the church, the body of which he is the Savior" (Eph. 5:23). This transforms the "great mystery" (v. 32) of Christian marriage into something "prophetic," where husband and wife "prefigure the second creation, the whole New Adam, which is anticipated in them."[4] In Martin Luther's view, it was in Christian marriage that we gained a taste of life in Eden before the fall. The man who married would find in his wife a nest or home, "a kind of faint image and remnant of that blessed living-together."[5]

In another way, this bond of husband and wife also *prefigures* the Trinity. Their "fellowship of love" based on spiritual equality also involves the willing submission of wife to husband, through which they find unity. So too, the Son and the Holy Spirit, who with their unique roles are coequal with the Father, find their origin and unity in submission to the Father.[6]

This vision of marriage simply cannot be confined to an ideological grid of the sort assumed in *From Culture Wars to Common Ground*. It exists in an altogether different dimension, one fitted into the whole pageant of redemption.

3. See Stephen Miletic, *One Flesh: Ephesians 5.22-24, 5.31, Marriage and the New Creation* (Rome: Editrice Pontifico Institute Biblico, 1988), pp. 111, 116.

4. Jean-Jacques von Allmen, *Pauline Teaching on Marriage* (London: Faith Press, 1963), pp. 47-48.

5. Martin Luther, "Lectures on Genesis."

6. Germain Grisez, *The Way of the Lord Jesus*, vol. 2: *Living a Christian Life* (Quincy, Ill.: Franciscan Press, 1993), p. 614; and Paul N. Check, *"Wives: Be Subject to Your Husbands": The Authority of the Husband According to the Magisterium* (Rome: Pontifico Ateneo Della Santa Croce, 1998), pp. 11, 54-55.

Problem Three

A third problem with the book's argument is that it devalues Christian love. The book describes a tension between the behavioral models of "self-sacrifice" and "equal regard," largely abandoning the former as unwarranted by Scripture and embracing the latter as the correct Christian choice. As the authors explain (p. 273): "We begin by boldly asserting that love as mutuality or equal regard, rather than love as self-sacrifice, is the core of Christian love in both life in general and in families." The book then charts a broad retreat from self-denial in favor of mutually satisfying self-fulfillment. Marital love comes to rest on "premoral values and goods" — food, clothing, pleasant friendships, sexual pleasure, recreation, and so forth, instead of any renunciation of self. With great reluctance, I will pass over the obvious rejoinders (Where do the Christian martyrs or Mother Teresa fit into this? Can marriage survive on an ethos not far removed from the "Four Way Test" of the Rotary Club?[7]) to pose another question: Even if one admits the inadequacy of "self-sacrifice" as a guide to normal life, is "mutual self-fulfillment" the only other possibility?

Even for the great majority who will fall short of sainthood, other vocabulary might be employed. Phrases that come to mind include altruism, sharing that grows out of love, and selfless giving. Or why not employ the rich term "complementarity"? In regard to the bond of marriage, it allows for equality *and* variety to co-exist without imposing a chilling uniformity. Instead, it creates a dynamic where selfless giving by both partners has a synergistic effect, where the whole becomes something greater than its parts. In his commentary on "the dignity of women," Pope Pius XII explained the phrase this way: "The Creator with His wonderful ways of bringing harmony out of variety has established a common destiny for all mankind, but He has also given the two sexes different and complementary functions, like two roads leading to the same destination."[8] Complementarity implies the *surrender* of each to the other, so that the couple together might be one complete being.

7. The Rotary Four Way Test reads: "Is it the truth? Is it fair to all concerned? Will it build good will and better friendship? Is it beneficial to all concerned?"

8. Pius XII, "The Dignity of Women" *(Con vivo gradimento), The Pope Speaks 3* (spring 1957): 370; in Check, *"Wives: Be Subject,"* p. 2.

Problem Four

In addition, the book's historiography (pp. 60-69; chapter 9) leads it toward an, at best, incomplete understanding of the relation of the family to the industrial economy. Are we to believe that some version of the "companionate family" was in fact the family model preferred by Jesus? The authors do not formally embrace the term "companionate family" (it is mentioned only briefly, on pages 259-60), yet their model of "equal regard" is, in fact, quite close to the "companionate" family model first developed by William Ogburn in the 1920s. As E. W. Burgess and H. J. Locke explained in 1945, the "companionship family" has shed most of its pre-modern economic, security, and education functions, and has refocused on "the mutual affection, the sympathetic understanding, and the comradeship of its members."[9] This seems almost identical to the authors' contemporary call for a family of "equal regard," defined as a husband-wife bond characterized by "mutual respect, affection, practical assistance, and justice." Locke and Burgess showed that such a family model is ideally suited to an individualistic, market-oriented society; it *presumes* that all adults will be active in the public sphere and that the family will be transformed from a basic socioeconomic institution into a psychological device focused on individual well-being.

The authors of *From Culture Wars to Common Ground* rightly point to those teachings of Jesus that questioned the social conventions of his time. Even in light of Jesus' pointed critique of certain aspects of the patriarchal family, however, the end result was *not* a "companionship" family rooted in "equal regard." Even the nuclear unit found in Palestine villages two thousand years ago remained a tightly integrated economic body, one focused on household self-sufficiency in food production, education, and other crucial functions. I suggest that the model family to be found in the social theology of Jesus and "the Jesus movement" would be far closer in structure to the "yeoman farm" families of early-nineteenth-century America, or to the Amish or Bruderhof movements of today, than to the family system of 1950 Levittown or 2003 Manhattan. The goal would be for the father to gain sufficient remuneration that women and children could *leave* the factories, return

9. E. W. Burgess and H. J. Locke, *The Family* (New York: American Book Company, 1945), pp. 651, 654-72.

home, and restore some semblance of family autonomy in the new industrial milieu.[10]

Problem Five

On page 153 the authors write, "Equal regard, as we define it, is a strenuous ethic." Might this be true in ways they do not really intend? As I read the explanations, an ethic of "equal regard" will involve a daily, even hourly, calculation of gain, loss, and balance in relationship to one's spouse, a vastly complicated calculus of keeping score, always asking, "Am I ahead?" "Am I behind?" A sample of this tense effort at a material measure of equity is found on page 284, where we read, "It follows that she [the wife] too should have access to the power, financial capacity, and social respect required *to make certain* that this sacrificial love is not exploited." Is this focus on power and money within marriage really the New Testament gospel message? Would it be so in *any* area of life? For *men* or *women?*

Problem Six

Does the family, including ancestors and posterity, have institutional claims of its own that are separate from those of the individuals who make it up? If the family is merely the sum of its current parts, then an ethic of "mutual regard" focused heavily on each individual's status should work reasonably well. But if the family is, in fact, "the fundamental unit of society," where the whole is greater than the sum of its parts, then "mutual regard" will prove to be wholly inadequate. By definition, it cannot transcend its individualistic forms.

---

10. See J. Humphries, "The Working Class Family," in *The Family in Political Thought*, ed. Jean Bethke Elshtain (Amherst: University of Massachusetts Press, 1982), pp. 197-222; and A. C. Carlson, "Gender, Children, and Social Labor: Transcending the 'Family Wage' Dilemma," *Journal of Social Issues* 52, no. 3 (1996): 137-61.

Problem Seven

The volume's reliance on psychological terminology and its quest for "new language" actually get in the way of the poetry and mystery of Scripture. On page 276, we read, "The ancient teaching that in marriage husband and wife *become one flesh* can receive new meaning if enriched by the idea that marriage is a covenant of intersubjective dialogue that enacts love as equal regard." But do the phrases, "a covenant of intersubjective dialogue" and "enacts love as equal regard" truly enrich the extraordinary term, "one flesh"? Even in terms of linguistic economy, I believe that the author of Genesis wins out.

A Final Problem

Finally, if the goal of the authors is truly "renewing families" (p. 2), they should take pause at the fact (reported on pp. 280-81) that "mutuality" or "equal regard" is actually the dominant ethos in the most enfeebled, demographically challenged Christian denominations, Episcopalianism and Presbyterianism. Even using official denominational numbers, which tend to overstate membership, both church bodies reported steadily declining numbers throughout the 1980s and 1990s; Sunday school enrollments suffered the most. Viewed empirically, it appears that the ethic of "equal regard," whatever its virtues for some individuals, is not conducive to evangelism, to the appearance of children in church, or to the renewal of families.

CHAPTER 9

Headship and the Bible

W. Robert Godfrey

WHAT DOES the Bible teach about headship in the human community? Some defenders of "equal regard" assume tensions or even contradictions within the biblical teaching and claim that they are following the genuinely Christian trajectory of the biblical text. Others seem content to argue in effect that the Bible is a big book and that many interpretations are possible and, implicitly, equally valid.[1]

By contrast this essay builds on the historic Christian conviction of nearly two centuries that although the Bible is a big book written over many centuries by numerous authors, it is the inspired revelation of God and is consistent internally in its teaching on headship and related issues.[2] An examination of the actual teaching of the Bible will show this consistency to exist in the Bible's teaching about men and women. Relevant passages from the Bible will be quoted rather fully in

1. Several essays in this volume take such positions in claiming the support of the Bible for their egalitarian position on the relationships of men and women. Don Browning writes of the "direction" of the message of the Bible. Bonnie Miller-McLemore writes of the "prophetic heritage" of the Bible. Mary Stewart Van Leeuwen refers to the "mixed voices" found in Paul. Such interpretations of the Bible are more asserted than argued. The essay by Allan Carlson challenges the tendency to use biblical texts out of context. This essay tries to demonstrate the consistency of the Bible in answer to such assertions.

2. This conviction about the Bible is the historic position of both Roman Catholic and Protestant ideologies. Lisa Cahill and Daniel Cere as representatives of Roman Catholic theology in this volume do not clearly relate their positions to the Bible, resting more on the authority of the magisterium or the historical development of dogma. Yet even in relation to these authorities little is made of historic Roman Catholic teaching or the present practice of excluding women from the priesthood.

the conviction that the clarity and consistency of the biblical message is more apparent on reading the words of the texts than on just seeing textual references.

The first clear teaching of the Bible is that men and women are equal in terms of value and dignity in creation and in redemption. Women and men were created in the image of God to enjoy in that unique status a blessed communion and fellowship with God: "So God created man in his own image, in the image of God he created him; male and female he created them" (Gen. 1:27).[3] Then God gave man and woman together as his image-bearers the responsibility to be fruitful and exercise dominion on the earth (Gen. 1:28). Though Paul teaches in Romans 5 that Adam has a unique responsibility for the fall of mankind into sin, both Adam and Eve sinned against God and hid from God (Gen. 3:7, 8). Further, men and women equally share in the redemptive and restorative work of Christ, as declared by Paul:

> You are all sons of God through faith in Christ Jesus, for all of you who were baptized into Christ have clothed yourselves with Christ. There is neither Jew nor Greek, slave nor free, male nor female, for you are all one in Christ Jesus. If you belong to Christ, then you are Abraham's seed, and heirs according to the promise. (Gal. 3:26-29)

In Christ, women are as fully the heirs of salvation and the sons of God as are men. The events of Pentecost also demonstrate that men and women are equally members of Messiah's new age. The prophet Joel had looked forward to the messianic kingdom:

> Then you will know that I am in Israel,
>   that I am the LORD your God,
>   and that there is no other;
> never again will my people be shamed.
> And afterward,
>   I will pour out my Spirit on all people.
> Your sons and daughters will prophesy,
>   your old men will dream dreams,
>   your young men will see visions.

3. Biblical passages in this essay are quoted from the New International Version of the Bible.

> Even on my servants, both men and women,
>> I will pour out my Spirit in those days. . . .
> And everyone who calls
>> on the name of the LORD will be saved. . . ."
>
> (Joel 2:27-29, 32)

The fulfillment of this prophecy is described in Acts 2 where the Spirit comes upon all of the church and all speak in tongues (v. 4). This showed that all had the Spirit of Christ in the church of Christ and that all who had called on the name of the Lord were saved.

The second clear teaching of the Bible is that men and women stand in a complementary relationship to one another. They are not identical, a fact certainly made clear from creation. God made man and woman to be one flesh, neither complete without the other. God presented Eve to Adam not as an inferior or a superior but as a suitable helper (Gen. 2:18) who would end Adam's loneliness and with him people and subdue the earth. Yet the Genesis account makes clear that while the work of the man and the work of the woman are related, they are not identical. Adam had a primary responsibility in working the ground and Eve a primary responsibility for bearing children. That point is made in their names: "Adam" echoes the Hebrew word for "ground" and "Eve" is related to the Hebrew word for "life." Similarly, their primary roles are clarified in the curses God pronounced after the fall: man is cursed in his working of the ground and woman is cursed in childbirth.

The complementary character of their roles did not mean, however, that women were narrowly restricted to work as mothers in the Old Testament. Consider the picture of the ideal wife presented in Proverbs 31. This woman is called the wife of noble character (v. 10) who brings her husband good (v. 12), yet the area of her activity is wide indeed. She prepares and weaves wool and flax for clothing (vv. 13, 19, 22, 24); she gathers and prepares food (v. 15); she administers a household of servants (vv. 15, 27); she negotiates for and buys a field and plants a vineyard (v. 16); she earns profits at trade (vv. 18, 24); she cares for the poor (v. 20); she uses her wisdom to instruct others (v. 26).

This Old Testament family ideal remained an ideal that did not embrace everyone. Some men and women were poor or childless. Some were unmarried, divorced, or widowed. Fundamentally the same situation prevails in the New Testament. The normal expectation is that men and women will be married and have complementary roles in the family: "Then they [the older women] can train the younger women to love their husbands and children, to be self-controlled and pure, to be busy at home, to be kind, and to be subject to their husbands, so that no one will malign the word of God" (Titus 2:4-5). But the New Testament also clearly states that serving God may mean one must remain single as Jesus and some of the apostles did. Paul commends singleness for those called to live in that state for the sake of their service to God (1 Cor. 7:25-40).

Flowing from biblical teachings on the equality of men and women in dignity and value, and on the complementarity of men and women in various responsibilities, we find also in the Scriptures a leadership role for men in the family and church. These strands of biblical teaching are not in conflict with one another but reflect a coherent vision: men and women are of equal worth before God, ordinarily needing each other to live their lives, and having distinct responsibilities before God.

Genesis points to this male leadership in that Adam was created before Eve (Gen. 2:20-24) and that Adam named Eve (Gen. 3:20).[4] Leadership is given to man to begin a new family: "For this reason a man will leave his father and mother and be united to his wife, and they will become one flesh" (Gen. 2:24). This leadership exists before the fall into sin. Paul makes this point explicitly as the foundation of his prohibition against authoritative teaching by women in the church: "For Adam was formed first, then Eve" (1 Tim. 2:13).

Some claim that male leadership is the product of the fall and cite Genesis 3:16 to substantiate that: "Your desire will be for you husband, and he will rule over you." But to claim that male leadership begins with the fall is to ignore the evidence of leadership before the fall and to misunderstand Genesis 3:16. The curse is not that "he will rule over you," although in this fallen world it is all too easy for leadership to become oppressive and tyrannical. The curse is that "your desire will be

---

4. Van Leeuwen suggests that the key to understanding the Bible's teachings on men and women is to start with the story of creation rather than with Paul. Such a starting point is indeed a good one, but she ignores the information found in the creation story that points to male leadership.

for your husband." The rare word there translated as "desire" is found also in Genesis 4:7 where God says to Cain, "If you do what is right, will you not be accepted? But if you do not do what is right, sin is crouching at your door; it desires to have you, but you must master it." The curse on the woman is that she must live with the sinful desire to dominate her husband tyrannically, a desire that the godly woman will resist.

Male leadership is pervasive in the Old and New Testaments. Man is called the head of the woman: "Now I want you to realize that the head of every man is Christ, and the head of the woman is man, and the head of Christ is God. . . . For man did not come from woman, but woman from man" (1 Cor. 11:3, 8). The husband clearly is seen as the leader of the family: "Wives, submit to your husbands as to the Lord. For the husband is the head of the wife as Christ is the head of the church, his body, of which he is the Savior. Now as the church submits to Christ, so also wives should submit to their husbands in everything" (Eph. 5:22-24). Peter teaches the same:

> Wives, in the same way be submissive to your husbands so that, if any of them do not believe the word, they may be won over without words by the behavior of their wives, when they see the purity and reverence of your lives. . . . For this is the way the holy women of the past who put their hope in God used to make themselves beautiful. They were submissive to their own husbands, like Sarah, who obeyed Abraham and called him her master. You are her daughters if you do what is right and do not give way to fear. (1 Pet. 3:1-2, 5, 6)

The obedience to which wives are called in these texts is not a grievous burden when balanced by the love and care a Christian husband is to show his wife. "Husbands, love your wives, just as Christ loved the church and gave himself up for her to make her holy. . . . In this same way, husbands ought to love their wives as their own bodies. He who loves his wife loves himself. After all, no one ever hated his own body, but he feeds and cares for it, just as Christ does the church" (Eph. 5:25-26, 28-29). And again Peter, "Husbands, in the same way be considerate as you live with your wives, and treat them with respect as the weaker partner and as heirs with you of the gracious gift of life" (1 Peter 3:7).

The duties of husbands and wives found in Ephesians, the Pastoral Epistles, and 1 Peter resonate with the whole of the New Testament, and the key background for these duties is found not in Aristotle (as several writers in this volume seem to indicate) but in the Old Testament — both in the story of creation and in discussions of the roles of women, such as Proverbs 31.[5] Indeed, the call for Christian husbands to treat their wives with self-sacrificing love has no connection with Aristotle at all.

The Bible teaches male leadership in the church with equal clarity. For example, Paul wrote that "A woman should learn in quietness and full submission. I do not permit a woman to teach or to have authority over a man; she must be silent" (1 Tim. 2:11-12). The context in this text is the church as a worshiping community and its officers (1 Tim. 2 and 3). Women are not restricted from all teaching or enjoined to silence in all places. Rather, they are not to enter the authoritative teaching office of the church. Paul makes the same point in his first letter to the Corinthians:

> For God is not a God of disorder but of peace. As in all the congregations of the saints, women should remain silent in the churches. They are not allowed to speak, but must be in submission, as the Law says. If they want to inquire about something, they should ask their own husbands at home; for it is disgraceful for a woman to speak in the church. (1 Cor. 14:33-35)

Some note that in the same letter in which Paul silences women, he seems to give them the right to pray and prophesy in public: "And every woman who prays or prophesies with her head uncovered dishonors her head" (1 Cor. 11:5). Yet even in this context Paul stresses the need for women to cover their heads as "a sign of authority" (1 Cor. 11:10); in other words, as a sign that they recognize and express that they are under male authority. Also for Paul the work of the prophet is not an ordinary, ongoing office in the church, but an extraordinary

---

5. The essays of Browning and Gallagher, for example, refer explicitly to Aristotle, and neither of them sees the Old Testament as the critical foundation for the New Testament discussion of the family. Aristotle may well have influenced the medieval scholastic reading of the Bible, but the essays of this volume offer no evidence that Aristotle was a significant influence on New Testament writers.

work of the Spirit in the foundational age of the church. (See, for example, Ephesians 2:20.)

Male leadership is also seen in the specific qualifications given for office in the church: "Now the overseer must be above reproach, the husband of but one wife. . . . Deacons, likewise, are to be men worthy of respect" (1 Tim. 3:2, 8). "An elder must be blameless, the husband of but one wife" (Titus 1:6). Male leadership in the offices of the church does not mean, of course, that women have no important roles in the church: Jesus was accompanied by women and they gave the first witness to his resurrection; Paul spoke of women as fellow workers; Priscilla along with her husband Aquilla privately instructed Apollos in the faith (Acts 18:26). Their work is vital as a complement to that of the men in the church.

Historically, Reformed theology has made a distinction that is useful here, the distinction in the church between the special offices and the general office of believer. The special offices of minister, elder, and deacon seem closed to women, but the general office of work and service is for both men and women. Indeed, in the general office women may do everything that men may do.

In the Bible the leadership of the man in family and church is not just a matter of convenience or pragmatic arrangement but rests on a critical theological foundation.[6] Man has a representative function in the Bible, which does not know the radical individualism of modern culture but promotes a culture in which leaders represent and are responsible for the communities they lead. Such a vision of reality is reflected pervasively in the Bible. Joshua in his famous statement demonstrates this leadership and responsibility: "As for me and my household, we will serve the LORD" (Josh. 24:15). A similar perspective undergirds, for example, the tenth commandment: "You shall not covet

---

6. The theological issues discussed in this and the next paragraphs are largely ignored in the other essays of this volume, which is strange in light of the importance of these issues for the very essence of the Bible and Christianity. The defenders of an egalitarian approach also seem to give little attention to the question of the ways in which their views may be not so much a new theology as an accommodation to the prevailing views of contemporary culture. Perhaps the generally prophetic role of the Bible today is to confront the excesses of individualism and democratization which are ravaging institutions like the family. Gallagher's insights regarding the new socioeconomic context of the modern family are very valuable in this regard.

your neighbor's house. You shall not covet your neighbor's wife, or his manservant or maidservant, his ox or donkey, or anything that belongs to your neighbor" (Exod. 20:17). Does this commandment not apply to women or servants? Is it only for men who are leaders of households? Obviously not. But the commandment as it stands is a reminder of the representative function of male leaders for the community as a whole. Or consider Psalm 1: "Blessed is the man. . . ." In this introduction to the whole Psalter a specifically male noun is used, not a generic reference to humanity. Why? Not because women are not to live holy lives or love the law of God, but because man has a leading and representative function in humanity's relationship with God.

The representative leadership of man in the Bible has a yet deeper significance. Adam was not just the head of his family. Beyond that, he represented the whole human race in its relations with God. "In Adam's fall we sinned all," said the McGuffey reader. McGuffey was paraphrasing 1 Corinthians 15:22, "For as in Adam all die, so in Christ all will be made alive." As 1 Corinthians shows, a key to the meaning of the work of Christ is his representative headship of the new humanity. Paul develops that theme more fully in his letter to the Romans:

> Therefore, just as sin entered the world through one man, and death through sin, and in this way death came to all men, because all sinned. . . . But the gift is not like the trespass. For if the many died by the trespass of the one man, how much more did God's grace and the gift that came by the grace of the one man, Jesus Christ, overflow to the many! . . . Consequently, just as the result of one trespass was condemnation for all men, so also the result of one act of righteousness was justification that brings life for all men. For just as through the disobedience of the one man the many were made sinners, so also through the obedience of the one man the many will be made righteous. (Rom. 5:12, 15, 18-19)

According to the Bible the very meaning of the redemptive work of Christ rests on the foundation of representative male headship.

Often in the discussion of male headship, defenders of a modern idea of equality appeal to what they see as an analogy between male leadership in the Bible and slavery.[7] They argue that although the Bible

---

7. Van Leeuwen, for example, makes a brief comparison between slaves and women.

regulates the practice of slavery, slavery was later outlawed on the basis of biblical principles. So too, they argue, male headship can be eliminated as slavery was. But no actual parallel exists between male headship and slavery. In the first place, the institution of slavery is clearly a result of the fall and is not grounded in creation, whereas male headship *is* grounded in creation. In the second place, the Bible itself provides indications that slavery is a problematic institution. Paul sees the superiority of freedom over slavery: "Were you a slave when you were called? Don't let it trouble you — although if you can gain your freedom, do so" (1 Cor. 7:21). He also lists among gross sins "slave traders" (1 Tim. 1:10), although that word probably refers primarily to those who kidnap individuals and enslave them (cf. Rev. 18:13). Also in the tender letter to Philemon, a slave owner, about his slave Onesimus, Paul wrote,

> Perhaps the reason he was separated from you for a little while was that you might have him back for good — no longer as a slave, but better than a slave, as a dear brother. He is very dear to me but even dearer to you, both as a man and as a brother in the Lord.
>
> So if you consider me a partner, welcome him as you would welcome me. If he has done you any wrong or owes you anything, charge it to me. (Philemon vv. 15-18)

The call to recognize a slave as a fellow human and a brother did undermine the institution of slavery. No such language is found in the Bible for the liberation of women. The Bible does not see male headship as a bondage from which women need to be liberated.

Another argument sometimes made to blunt the teaching of the Bible on headship is that Jesus and his disciples for the sake of order did not criticize institutions and prejudices of the first century in relation to women. By implication, then, the advice of the New Testament to women is limited to only the first century, and later times can change that advice.[8] But in fact the New Testament records a number of instances in which Jesus and the apostles violated the norms of con-

---

8. A position somewhat like this is taken by Cere in his contention that first-century Christians tried to live out the lordship of Christ in the "institutions of the secular world" of their day. But the church and family were not institutions of the secular world in the first century. They were institutions carefully prepared in the Old Testament and regulated by apostolic authority in the New.

temporary Judaism. Jesus, for example, spoke privately to women. (Note how surprised his disciples were to find him alone speaking to the Samaritan woman, John 4:27, and how Jesus implicitly criticized them and their attitude when he called on them to be laborers gathering the harvest of lives for his kingdom.) Women were the first witnesses in the apostolic community to the resurrection of Jesus. Jesus and Paul encouraged women to study the faith and to serve the church in a variety of capacities. All of these violated accepted norms and roles for women in Judaism, but Jesus and Paul freely corrected those false ideas.

The teaching of the Bible about male leadership is, in fact, clear and consistent.[9] One of the great issues before the church today is whether the Bible will continue to function prophetically for the church and the world on this matter as on so many others. If Christians come to believe that the Bible is self-contradictory or can be interpreted to mean anything the interpreter wants, then the Bible will become a closed book for Christians. Why read the Bible if it is confused or confusing? If Christians adopt an approach to language or gender roles in our culture that makes the language and teaching of the Bible seem oppressive and sexist, then the Bible will be discarded as another product of male tyranny. These tendencies among Christians must be resisted especially by Protestants, one of whose founding declarations was *sola scriptura*. That slogan meant that the Bible alone was the reliable source of religious truth and reformation for the church. The church still needs the prophetic word of the Bible, in particular as it speaks on the issue of male leadership.

9. For fuller development of the kinds of arguments presented in this essay, see Werner Neuer, *Man and Woman in Christian Perspective* (Wheaton, Ill.: Crossway, 1991); John Piper and Wayne A. Grudem, eds., *Recovering Biblical Manhood and Womanhood: A Response to Evangelical Feminism* (Wheaton, Ill.: Crossway, 1991); and Andreas J. Köstenberger, Thomas R. Schreiner, and H. Scott Baldwin, eds., *Women in the Church* (Grand Rapids: Baker, 1995).

CHAPTER 10

Marriage, Subordination, and the Development of Christian Doctrine

Daniel Mark Cere

TODAY RADICALLY new questions are being raised within the Christian tradition concerning the nature of relations between the sexes: How is the long-standing tradition of one-sided subordination of wives to husbands compatible with an affirmation of the dignity, rights, and equality of women? On what moral grounds can one argue for the restriction of women to a domestic sphere governed by men?

The fact that the legitimacy of wifely subordination is no longer self-evident constitutes a genuinely new historical circumstance. Well into the modern period, as Merry Weisner points out, just about everybody — Protestants and Catholics, humanists and zealots, male and female reformers alike — affirmed the subordination of wives to their husbands.[1] Most emphasized the need to temper the husband's authority, morally and pastorally, but some form of domestic patriarchy was taken for granted as part of the natural order of social relations. The novelty of the question is at the root of much of our anxious and inconclusive study of biblical perspectives on relations between wives and husbands.

As Mary Stewart Van Leeuwen suggests in her essay, through her vivid image of dueling hands of Scripture poker, exegetical debates by themselves seldom offer clear or satisfactory resolutions to fundamentally new lines of questioning. Consider the lexical debates that have

---

1. Merry E. Weisner, "Family, Household, and Community," in *Handbook of European History, 1400-1600*, ed. Thomas A. Brady Jr., Heiko A. Oberman, and James D. Tracy (Leiden: E. J. Brill, 1994) p. 66; Merry E. Weisner, *Women and Gender in Early Modern Europe* (Cambridge: Cambridge University Press, 1993), chap. 1.

raged around the significance of *kephale,* the Greek term for "head." In 1954 Stephen Bedale published an article arguing that the term *kephale* did not carry the connotations of an office or institution of authority in first-century New Testament Greek. For two generations scholars have been debating this point.[2]

In evangelical circles this scholarly debate has established a battle line between advocates of a subordinationist ethic of spousal relations and those advocating a more egalitarian approach (though even some opponents of headship, like Carolyn Osiek, acknowledge that it is unlikely that *kephale* is devoid of connotations of authority).[3] Forty years after Bedale's essay, A. C. Perriman published a careful review of both lines of argument. He doubts whether a satisfactory resolution to the debate can be found, and certainly the years have produced no consensus on the question.[4]

Why the ongoing disagreement? The difficulty is due in part to the fact that this lexical debate is being driven by an underlying question foreign to the explicit concerns of Scripture, namely, whether the term "head" supports and reinforces a patriarchal order or whether it is, in effect, directing attention away from questions of authority. Does Christianity affirm, challenge, or — as Carolyn Osiek puts it in this volume — simply "assume" a patriarchal structure of authority in marriage?

2. Support for this thesis can be found in the work of Hans Conzelmann, Heinrich Schlier, Edward Schillebeeckx, and Rudolf Schnackenberg. More recently, this line of argument has been developed by Jerome Murphy O'Connor, R. S. Cervin, and Alvera Mickelsen. It has also, however, been subject to vigorous critique by Wayne Grudem and Joseph Fitzmeyer, who claim that the term can and does carry connotations of authority.

3. See Osiek's statement on p. 23 of this volume: "I think the critics are correct that most of the evidence does not support that interpretation as a general meaning." On the debate in general, see "Battle in the Lexicon," *Christianity Today* 31 (1987): 44-46.

4. Stephen Bedale, "The Meaning of *Kephale* in the Pauline Epistles," *Journal of Theological Studies* 5 (1954); R. S. Cervin, "Does *Kephale* ('Head') Mean 'Source' or 'Authority over' in Greek Literature? A Rebuttal," *Trinity Journal* 10 (1989); Joseph Fitzmyer, "Another Look at *Kephale* in 1 Cor. 11:3," *New Testament Studies* 34 (1989): 506-10; and "*Kephale* in 1 Cor. 11:3," *Interpretation* 47 (1993): 52-59; Wayne Grudem, "Does *Kephale* ('Head') Mean 'Source' or 'Authority over' in Greek Literature?" *Trinity Journal* 6 (1985): 38-52 and "The Meaning of *Kephale,*" *Trinity Journal* 11 (1990): 3-79; Beverly Mickelsen and Alvera Mickelsen, "What Does *Kephale* Mean in the New Testament?" in *Women, Authority, and the Bible,* ed. A. Mickelsen (Downers Grove, Ill.: InterVarsity, 1986), pp. 97-105; A. C. Perriman, "The Head of a Woman: The Meaning of *Kephale* in 1 Cor. 11:3," *Journal of Theological Studies* 45 (1994): 602-22.

Scripture's response to this puzzle appears to be stubbornly evasive. In Greco-Roman contexts, the content of the household codes focused on structures of authority and order between husband and wife, father and children, master and slaves. Hellenistic culture offered a variety of household codes from Aristotelian, Stoic, and Neo-Platonic sources. David Balch maintains that the household codes in Ephesians and Colossians clearly reflect the choice of an Aristotelian tradition of discourse on household management. The structure of Ephesians is similar to Aristotle's discussion of the household in Book One of the *Politics:* three pairs of social classes (husbands/wives, parents/children, masters/slaves), with the classes reciprocally related, and one class in each pair ruling while the other is to be ruled.[5]

New Testament authors are thus engaging a problematic that received a number of distinct formulations in the classical world, and, in the case of the codes in Ephesians and Colossians, the author seems to be drawn to one particular formulation — the Aristotelian household code. There is nothing particularly new or remarkable in this discovery. A common designation for biblical household codes in contemporary scholarship is *haustafeln,* a term coined by Luther. In his exposition of Psalm 127:1, "Unless the LORD builds the house," Luther states that the term *haustafeln* "refers to everything that goes on inside the house, which in German we call 'managing the household.'" He readily admits, however, that this is equivalent to Aristotle's discussion of the household economy, *oeconomia.*[6] The parallels between these two traditions were common knowledge.[7]

---

5. See David Balch's discussion of the debate in *Let Wives Be Submissive: The Domestic Code in 1 Peter* (Chico, Calif.: Scholars Press, 1981), chap. 1. See also David Balch, "Household Codes," in *Greco-Roman Literature and the New Testament,* ed. David Aune (Atlanta: Scholars Press, 1988), pp. 25-50; J. F. Crouch, *The Origin and Intention of the Corinthian Haustafel* (Gottingen: FRLANT, 1972); and W. Schrage, "Zur Ethik der neutestamentliche Haustafel," *New Testament Studies* 21 (1975): 1-22.

6. Martin Luther, "Exposition of Psalm 127," in *Luther's Works,* vol. 45, ed. W. Brandt (Philadelphia: Fortress, 1962).

7. In the opening section of his commentary on Ephesians 5, Aquinas points out that this text reflects the household order depicted by Aristotle in Book One of the *Politics.* Aquinas uses the Aristotelian analysis of household relations to interpret the depiction of authority relations between husband and wife in Ephesians 5. (Thomas Aquinas, *Commentary on Saint Paul's Epistle to the Ephesians,* trans. Matthew Lamb [Albany: Magi, 1966].)

James Dunn has pointed out what Don Browning, Carolyn Osiek, and other equal-regard advocates in this volume also call our attention to: we can draw at least one firm conclusion from this scriptural research, namely that the New Testament household codes are definitely not "a distinctively Christian creation."[8] Nonetheless, the New Testament is clearly willing to engage the classical concerns about the political structuring of the household. But what does this engagement signify?

There are a number of possibilities. First, it could be seen as the promotion of a patriarchal *kerygma* (revelation/proclamation). Texts like Ephesians 5 might be baptizing a certain form of political relations within the household. For some commentators the New Testament household codes sharpen emphasis on male authority by putting forward a doctrine or theology of patriarchy in which the leadership of husband/father is clothed in the sacred authority of Christ. This clothing may chasten and redeem the hard edges of patriarchal authority by grounding it in *agape,* the sacrificial love of Christ. Since this *agape* love bears the insignia of the priestly kingship of Christ, it brings authority and submission into the very heart of the spousal relationship. Thus, a purged and baptized patriarchy receives a very firm theological grounding.

In order to make this theological affirmation of patriarchal order work, however, one has to lean hard on the theologically rich household code of Ephesians 5:21-33 and to argue that a basic intention of the Pauline analogy between husband/wife and Christ/church is to drive home the analogous patterns of one-sided authority and submission in both relationships. This approach skates over thin ice in two ways: first, the vein of biblical material supporting this strong line of interpretation is not particularly thick; and second, the reading of the head/body analogy as an attribution of Christ's kingly authority to the husband can be challenged.

A second possibility is that the New Testament household codes may be evidence of a failed egalitarian *kerygma.* Elisabeth Schüssler Fiorenza argues for the existence of a radical egalitarian ethic in the early Jesus movement. It is true that Jesus challenged patriarchy and

---

8. James D. G. Dunn, "The Household Rules in the New Testament," in *The Family in Theological Perspective,* ed. Stephen C. Barton (Edinburgh: T&T Clark, 1996), p. 53.

that the early Pauline tradition sustained this challenge. This egalitarian *kerygma* remains, however, a promise unfulfilled. The pervasive patriarchal attitudes of the ancient world presented a formidable cultural fact for Christians trying to be respectable citizens and to integrate into Greco-Roman society. David Balch and Elisabeth Schüssler Fiorenza argue that these factors placed enormous pressure on the egalitarianism of the Jesus movement and early Pauline Christianity.[9] They claim that the New Testament codes represent early accommodations and compromises to mainstream Hellenistic culture; in other words, in the post-Pauline period, Christians caved in to cultural pressures and abandoned the egalitarian thrust of the gospel in order to meet the expectations of the dominant patriarchal order. Van Leeuwen makes this argument in this volume when she writes, "In the midst of a patriarchal society already inclined to see this new Jewish-messianic sect as at best somewhat weird and at worst subversive of the political order, some concessions to local gender norms were essential."

There is a problem with this argument — that the household codes reveal the collapse of an early egalitarian *kerygma* — as well, however. Does the New Testament really offer much evidence for these profound tensions and contests over gender relations? Are such readings anachronistic — projections of current conflicts and debates onto the distant past?

A third reading is possible — a conspiratorial egalitarian *kerygma*. According to this theory, the gospel does not disown lay cultures but engages them in their historical particularity and presses for their re-creation. The strategy for social reform is to enter into everyday relationships and to effect "transformation from within" by inserting radically new theological leaven that subverts the inner core of patriarchal codes. Mary Stewart Van Leeuwen in this volume draws our attention to a comparison with slavery: "Just as Paul does not call for the sudden overturning by Christians of slavery as an institution, but undermines it from within by urging both slaves and masters to treat each other as brothers in Christ, so too for the sake of social order and successful evangelism he advises the recipients of his letters to play along with some of the local norms of patriarchy even as he proclaims that in Christ, 'There is no longer Jew or Greek, there is no lon-

9. For example, David Balch, "Household Codes," pp. 32-33, 36.

ger slave or free, there is no longer male or female, for all of you are one in Christ Jesus.'" Likewise Carolyn Osiek and Don Browning argue that the New Testament suggests a radical rethinking of household order along the lines of an egalitarian sacrificial love ethic rather than the agonistic honor-shame codes dominant in the classical world. As Browning puts it, the "trajectory" of early Christianity is away from patriarchy. The present task of Christian theology," he argues, is thus "to complete the early church's critique of male headship" and "finish the task of implementing its direction toward a marriage ethic of equal regard."

This third interpretation implies that the apostolic authors had a fairly astute grasp of the underlying substructures of patriarchal order and a remarkably prescient strategy for sabotaging this cultural matrix. While this is an attractive line of reasoning, nevertheless, it is not clear that this interpretation adequately meets the challenge presented by the first model. That early Christianity calls us to love our neighbor (or our wife) as ourself is indisputable, but is this kind of love as inconsistent with all hierarchy as the advocates of equal regard believe? A chastened patriarchalism collapses agonistic honor-shame codes and reconfigures a subordinationist pattern of gender relations within the context of an ethos of sacrificial love. To note, as equal-regard advocates do, that this loving sacrifice is made in the interests of union (or mutuality) and not for its own sake does not change the fundamental reality: The image of Christ, as sacrificial lover *and* Lord, underscores the contention that authority and *agape* can be profoundly interwoven.

Scripture is thus inconclusive on this point, because we are asking St. Paul to answer for us questions that he clearly never asked himself. Where does that leave the Christian theologian, or for that matter the Christian spouse? New developments in Christian doctrine can be triggered by new historical circumstances, by the fact that — as John Henry Newman put it — we raise "great questions" that bear upon "the subject-matter of which Scripture treats" but that are not explicitly formulated, posed, or answered within Scripture itself. They are questions, Newman insists, "so real, so practical, that they must be answered," yet they "find no solution on the surface of Scripture, nor indeed under the surface in the case of most men, however long and diligent might be their study of it." New questions imply the need to formulate responses that must, of necessity, go beyond the conceptual horizons of Scripture.[10]

Newman would argue that we cannot hope to "find an answer" within Scripture or tradition to questions they do not pose. We can, however, judiciously consider the testimony of both Scripture and tradition and make a judgment. Whatever judgment we arrive at will constitute an "addition" to the conceptual horizons of Scripture and tradition. In judging such a potential new development the key question is this: Will this addition preserve and enhance the acquisitions gained in the development of Christian doctrine or will it obscure, corrupt, and reverse them?

Certainty is not easily won in such a process. Newman warns that all historical inquiry is "delicate and doubtful . . . depending for its success or failure far more on the individual exercising it than on rules which can be laid down."[11] Nevertheless, his *Essay on the Development of Christian Doctrine* (1845) does attempt to establish theoretical procedures for analyzing the development of historical traditions. Newman devised a set of seven tests to assess the fit of a particular addition with the course of a historical tradition. Applying just one of Newman's tests — continuity of principle — suggests a few lines of inquiry that might prove fruitful.

10. John Henry Newman, *Essay on the Development of Christian Doctrine*, 1878 ed. (London: Longmans, 1909), 60, 337. If the lack of explicit biblical evidence counted against new formulations of doctrine, then, Newman warns, much of orthodox christology, and probably all Trinitarian theology, would have to be jettisoned. Newman's first work, *The Arians of the Fourth Century*, argued that Arius's stand against Nicea was essentially a stance of conservative biblicism. Arius wanted to restrict the range of theological discourse on the divinity of Christ and to cling to the strict limits of biblical language. The question posed by Nicea — "Is the Son one in being with the Father?" — presented a new and deeper questioning of the biblical vision of God. It was a line of questioning that was not explicitly posed by Scripture itself. By insisting on older formulations and resisting an affirmative response to the Nicean question, Arius stood on Scripture and rejected the concept of the Son's true divinity. A dogged conservatism can be just as problematic as a facile liberalism for the development of Christian doctrine.

11. John Henry Newman, *Essay on the Development of Christian Doctrine* (1845; reprint, Middlesex: Penguin, 1974), p. 239.

"Continuity of Principle": Hermeneutical Strategies

Using the principle of continuity, the job of the theologian is to sift through the tradition to try to identify certain principles or methods that are consistently applied in the exploration of a particular subject matter. These are what Newman defines as the regulative "axioms," "instruments," or procedural norms which govern the formulation of a stance in the Christian tradition on specific topics.[12] So, for example, in the development of the doctrine of the incarnation, Newman argues that certain perspectives on the relationship between faith and reason, the nature of theological discourse, and modes of biblical interpretation will have a "formal connexion" to a course of doctrinal development.[13]

Applying this test to our present task — the question of male headship in marriage — requires us to identify the common hermeneutical procedures that have been employed within the Christian tradition to facilitate the exploration of conjugal relations and the household order. If Newman is right, these procedures should suggest real clues and strategies for engaging the new questions before us.

Patristic and Medieval Perspectives

What are the axioms or principles of marital relations, in Newman's sense, that form the core of the Christian tradition? Augustine and Aquinas are two seminal figures in the crystallization of patristic and medieval thinking about marriage and gender issues. In the *City of God*, Augustine offers a brief discussion of the question of authority within the home. The context is an ethical reflection on how rational and just political authority should serve the interests of the governed. The achievement of "domestic peace" and "harmony" requires authority and subordination; however, authority should be exercised "for the interests of others." In this sense, "even those who give orders are the servants of those whom they appear to command," for "they do not give orders because of a lust for domination but from a dutiful concern for

12. Newman, *Essay on the Development* (1878 ed.), pp. 178ff, 326.
13. Newman, *Essay on the Development* (1878 ed.), pp. 344-45; 323-54.

the interests of others, not with pride in taking precedence over others, but with compassion in taking care of others."[14] Augustine advocates an ethical paternalism that follows in lockstep with the best of Aristotelian thinking on the patriarchal structure of household management.[15]

There are two points to note about Augustine's discussion. First, it is a negligible aspect of his reflections on marriage, and of no theological interest to him. His theological interests surface only in his discussion of the fundamental goods of marriage and his exploration of marriage's *sacramentum,* its radical indissolubility. Second, he does not attempt to transpose this ethical or political patriarchalism into more theological modes of discourse. The politics of household management, in his view, deals with the natural order of social life.

Likewise, Aquinas's discussion of conjugal authority is carefully framed and qualified; obedience is a moral and political virtue, not a theological one.[16] It concerns the just deference which we owe to any legitimate authority.[17] In his exploration of this virtue, Aquinas turns to a question implied by the language of the Pauline household codes, namely "whether subjects are bound to obey their superiors *in all things.*" He concludes that superiors are not to be obeyed in all things "but only in certain things and in a particular way." Thus, Paul's exhortation to wives to be subject to their husbands "in all things" demands careful interpretation.

Aquinas condemns unconditional obedience as an irresponsible act and argues that "when the Apostle says *in all things,* he refers to matters within the sphere of a father's or master's authority." This sphere of authority concerns only the "disposal of actions" that are "done externally by means of the body." It does not require subjection of "the will," nor is one "bound to obey another man in matters touching the

---

14. Augustine, *City of God,* 19.14.

15. When Augustine turns to a discussion of the authority of masters over slaves, however, he throws in a curve that is foreign to Aristotelian thought. He argues that the willing submission of "devout men" is subversive: "if they cannot be set free by their masters, they themselves may thus make their slavery, in a sense, free, by serving not with slyness or fear, but with the fidelity of affection, until all injustice disappears and all human lordship and power is annihilated, and God is all in all" (*City of God* 19.15).

16. Aquinas, *Summa Theologica* IIa.IIae, q. 104, art. 3.

17. Aquinas, *Summa Theologica* IIa.IIae, q. 104, art. 2.

nature of the body, for instance in those relating to the support of the body or the begetting of children." He also points out that children are not required to obey their parents "in the question of contracting marriage or of remaining in the state of virginity or the like."[18]

Furthermore, Aquinas states that the relationship of husband and wife in marriage should not entail servile obedience. The creation of Eve from the side of Adam signifies a certain equality which allows for "the social union of man and woman" rather than a servile subjugation of the woman to man.[19] He argues that there are two types of rule in the marriage relationship. With the advent of sin *(post peccatum)* authority became corrupt and self-serving. The wife was reduced to a "servile" position, ministering to the needs and interests of her husband. Aquinas does, however, envisage an authority that can be just. In the state of "original justice" *(ante peccatum)* authority is "civil" rather than "servile." In a civil society, the governor exercises authority for the welfare and benefit of his subjects and for the "common good," not for his own personal benefit. Authentic paternal authority must serve the subject rather than the one in authority.[20] In this discussion, Aquinas is employing the best intuitions of the Aristotelian approach to household order.

Aquinas's conception of the nature of the matrimonial bond does, however, begin to put some pressure on this subordinationist ethic. Taking "one flesh" as the starting point leads Aquinas toward mutuality in the marriage bond. He argues that there is a fundamental equality in the "unity and diversity of relation" which produces "the joining together of bodies and minds." This forges a relation of mutual belonging: "for the husband is the wife's husband and the wife is the husband's wife."[21] Aquinas argues that the equality of the husband and wife is exemplified in the marital act itself. While Aquinas admits a hierarchical ordering of conjugal relations, nevertheless he also insists that their complementary roles join in an equality of mutual obligations and rights. Charles Reid has explored the medieval transformation of Paul's concept of conjugal debt into the concept of conjugal

---

18. Aquinas, *Summa Theologica* IIa.IIae, q. 104, art. 5.
19. Aquinas, *Summa Theologica* Ia, 92, art. 3.
20. Aquinas, *Summa Theologica* Ia, 92, art. 3; *Commentary on Ephesians*, 216-23.
21. Aquinas, *Summa Theologica* IIa. Iiae, q. 44, art. 1.

rights *(ius)* and how this transformation served to equalize the spousal relationship.[22] Aquinas argues that this equality of rights and obligations extends beyond the bedroom into the actual "management of the household": "in both the marriage act and in the management of the household the husband is bound to the wife in all things pertaining to the husband, [and] the wife is bound to the husband in all things pertaining to the wife."[23]

While Aquinas's approach does offer a few significant departures from Aristotle's subordinationist reading of household management, nevertheless he is generally content to work within this framework. He reads little of theological significance into this order of subordination, however, and is content to briefly explore how this human social order described by Aristotle plays out in a Christian context. Indeed, he somewhat awkwardly tries to force this approach to the text upon his reader by re-translating the christocentric admonition to be subject to your husband "as to the Lord" into the more Aristotelian command to be subject to your husband "as to a master."[24] As with Augustine, Aquinas's theological interests are awakened only when he turns to the great questions of marriage: sacramentality, marital consent, indissolubility, and fidelity.

The sacramentality of marriage emerges as the centerpiece of Aquinas's teaching on marriage. Whether he is right is not germane here. What is significant is the way in which the focus on indissolu-

22. Charles J. Reid Jr., "The Canonistic Contribution to the Western Rights Tradition, A Historical Inquiry," *Boston College Law Review* 33 (1991): 80-91.

23. Aquinas, *Summa Theologica* IIa. IIae, q. 64, art. 5. This Thomistic mining of the egalitarian implications of conjugal rights and obligations finds its way into medieval discussions of the inner essence of marital love *(maritalis affectio)*. According to Michael Sheehan, medieval sermons and confessional manuals, not canon law and theology, offer the most "fruitful" sources for research into the medieval understanding of the "interior" life of conjugal love. One of the most developed reflections on marital love is offered by Guibert of Tournai, a Franciscan and a contemporary of Aquinas. Guibert believes that conjugal life should be marked by a deep and abiding friendship, by fidelity, and by an openness to mutual criticism. He provides a profoundly egalitarian definition of the nature of marital love: "a kind of love founded on partnership . . . the love which husband and wife owe to each other, because they are equals and partners" (quoted from "*Maritas affectio* Revisited," in Michael Sheehan's *Marriage, Family, and Law in Medieval Europe* [Toronto: University of Toronto Press, 1996], p. 276). Aquinas proves to be less adventuresome than his Franciscan counterpart.

24. Aquinas, *Commentary on Ephesians*, p. 217.

bility tends to sideline an emphasis on marital patriarchy. Calvin understood this well. In his sermon on Ephesians 5, he warned that any reading of the text in the light of the sacramentality of marriage obscures "Paul's meaning." The text must be "understood in its simplicity, that is to say, that God intends to inform man and wife what their duty and office is." For wives this means "to honour their husbands and to keep themselves in the subjection that God commanded."[25] Calvin warns that we cannot properly appreciate the biblically mandated order of authority in Ephesians if we allow its meaning to be absorbed by this novel doctrine of sacramentality. Calvin was right. Recognition of the sacramentality of marriage did tend to displace and marginalize theological concerns about household authority, and Aquinas is content to follow Aristotle's lead on the political ordering of the household. For Aquinas, the fundamental theological message of Ephesians 5 *is* the sacramentality of marriage. Whenever Ephesians 5 is cited in pre-Reformation doctrinal teaching (for example, the Council of Florence), the issue of sacramentality becomes the magnet around which theological reflection on the Christ/church and husband/wife analogy gravitates. The question of household order simply fades out of focus as an issue of theological concern.

An intriguing feature about the discussions of conjugal authority in the work of Augustine and Aquinas is that they do "imply" a response to Osiek's question, Did early Christians teach or merely presume male headship? For Augustine and Aquinas the question of woman's subordination is essentially an issue of political anthropology. Power relations naturally arise out of patterns of inequality in the human condition. A woman's state of subordination in marriage is not a theological assertion, but a natural pattern of social relationships that needs to be acknowledged and accommodated. There is no theological doctrine at stake here, but simply a debate about the political ethics of household order. Patriarchy is ethically affirmed only to the extent that it is presumed to be an inescapable dimension of social life. Given the nature of this approach, one could conclude that advancing new evidence to counter the presumption of female inferiority would force a reassessment about the subordinate status of women in marriage.

---

25. John Calvin, *Sermons on the Epistle to the Ephesians* (London: Banner of Truth Trust, 1973), pp. 606-7.

Early Modern Perspectives: Theologizing Subordination

Aquinas and Augustine are of course not the only Christian thinkers to reflect upon marriage. In the fourteenth and fifteenth centuries more decisively "theological" celebrations of patriarchal authority began to surface. Fifteenth-century marriage manuals give greater accent to the husband's central role in the home as lord, spiritual director, and educator. Renaissance Catholicism turns out to be far more ideologically patriarchal than medieval Catholicism. Less emphasis is placed on marital unanimity and fidelity and more on conjugal authority.[26]

In part, this development seems to be the result of the *devotio moderna* (modern devotion) movement's translation of monastic models of authority into the reformed "holy household." The male head is now entrusted with the religious functions and spiritual authority of the abbot.[27] Responsibilities for spiritual direction, teaching, and leading in family prayer are added to the husband's more traditional administrative tasks.[28] For the wife, obedience is no longer merely an ethically correct but a spiritually redeeming action. Marcus von Weida's influential rule for married laity emphasized that true unity in marriage could be attained only through wifely obedience: "The duty of the wife is to obey her husband as if he were her Prior and Prelate."[29] Marcus quotes Aquinas's contention that "nothing is more meritorious or pleasing to God than that one subjects oneself to the will of another for the sake of God"[30] — without informing readers that Aquinas is here discussing the vow of obedience in monastic life, not the nature of conjugal authority.

Devotio moderna writers also spearheaded the development of the cult of St. Joseph in their efforts to draw attention to the critical spiritual role of the paterfamilias. Until the late Middle Ages, Joseph is all

26. Silvana Vecchio, "The Good Wife," in *A History of Women in the West: Silences of the Middle Ages,* ed. Christiane Klapisch-Zuber (Cambridge, Mass.: Harvard University Press, 1992), pp. 130-31.

27. Robert James Bast, *Honor Your Fathers: Catechisms and the Emergence of a Patriarchal Ideology in Germany, 1400-1600* (Leiden: Brill, 1997), pp. 46-52, 58, 78.

28. Bast, *Honor Your Fathers,* p. 59.

29. Quoted in Bast, *Honor Your Fathers,* p. 71.

30. Aquinas, *Summa Theologica* IIa.IIae, q. 186, art. 5.

but invisible in Christian devotion, portrayed in art and literature as a feeble old man.[31] *Devotio moderna* authors transform Joseph into a virile provider and protector who takes command of the Holy Family and leads it victoriously through the trials of Jesus' early life. Pierre d'Ailly went so far as to argue that Mary, and even Christ in his human form, continue to remain under the loving spiritual headship of Joseph in heaven.[32]

In light of the restrained discussions of subordination put forward by Augustine and Aquinas, these more mystical views of conjugal authority appear to be inflated, excessive, and unbalanced. They are good examples of late medieval "theologism" — that misplaced theological pietism which runs roughshod over created reality in order to revel in the supernatural.[33]

None of this should come as a surprise since it is a truth almost universally acknowledged that in the Reformation patriarchy got cranked up a few notches.[34] Some have argued that this renewed emphasis on the divine nature of male authority in marriage was a residue of Catholic prejudice imported into Reformation theology, but that is more an apologetic stance than a historical argument.[35] The Reformers celebrated the critical religious role of the "holy households" as seminaries for the church. Men were encouraged to be holy patriarchs leading wife and children to God. The subordination of the wife and the headship of the husband were justified as a pivotal biblical mandate, not a mere judgment of practical reason based upon the natural moral order.

The theologization of conjugal authority that occurs within both the Catholic *devotio moderna* movement and the Reformation continues

31. Michael Herlihy, *Medieval Households* (Cambridge: Cambridge University Press, 1985), p. 127.

32. Herlihy, *Medieval Households,* p. 128.

33. Etienne Gilson, *The Unity of Philosophical Experience* (New York: Charles Scribners' Sons, 1937), chap. 2.

34. Stephen Ozment argues that this was a small price to pay for the renewal of marriage and family that the Reformers set in motion. (Steven Ozment, *When Fathers Ruled: Family Life in Reformation Europe* [Cambridge, Mass.: Harvard University Press, 1983].)

35. Bast, *Honor Your Fathers;* Joel F. Harrington, *Reordering Marriage and Society in Reformation Germany* (Cambridge: Cambridge University Press, 1995).

to find modern proponents. Some of the most important contributions in twentieth-century reflection were forged by the intimate intellectual collaborations of two famous theological couples — Karl Barth and Charlotte von Kirschbaum in Protestant theology and Hans Urs von Balthasar and Adrian von Speyr in Catholic theology.

In the Barthian approach, headship and subordination are grounded in a "Christological context" which defines the "irreversible order" of husband and wife; and it is upon this "secure theological knowledge" that we must rest "content."[36] There is not a whisper of interest in the secular roots and ethical form of the household codes. "We cannot avoid the fact that it is a real subordination," writes Barth. Kirschbaum argues that Ephesians specifies the meaning of Genesis 2:18 and forces one to "contest the allegation" that the "subjection of wives and women" is a "consequence and sign of sin." "God created her a woman and in doing so assigned to her a position of subordination," she writes.[37] The universal submission of all Christians to the Lord is specified in a unique way for women — "it is they, in contrast to men, who in their natural position as wives in relation to husbands reflect the position of Christians, that is, of the church, in relation to their Lord."[38] The woman's submission becomes a sign of the submission that characterizes the church as a whole.[39]

Similar views can be found in Catholic thought, and we will look just briefly at Adrian von Speyr. In her commentary *The Letter to the Ephesians,* she offers a similar theological affirmation of conjugal subordination. For Speyr the "entire relationship" of husband and wife is completely shaped and modeled on the relationship of Christ and the church. There is no sense of the limits of analogy in her discussion. She writes that

> obedience characterizes the whole existential attitude of the woman . . . marriage appears as a sort of extension to her husband

36. Quoted from George Tavard, *Woman in Christian Tradition* (Notre Dame, Ind.: University of Notre Dame Press, 1973), pp. 178-80.

37. Charlotte von Kirschbaum, *The Question of Woman: The Collected Writings of Charlotte von Kirschbaum,* trans. John Shepherd, ed. and with an intro. by Eleanor Jackson (Grand Rapids: Eerdmans, 1996), p. 66.

38. Kirschbaum, *The Question of Woman,* pp. 63-64.

39. Kirschbaum, *The Question of Woman,* pp. 88-89.

of her obedience vis-à-vis the Lord. . . . The man reveals to her the Lord; in him and behind him she sees the Lord.[40]

In Speyr as in Barth and Kirschbaum, therefore, the authority relationship between husband and wife is transfigured from a natural political relationship with clearly defined limits and boundaries into a profoundly theological and redemptive event that exceeds such boundaries

Such approaches, however, are predicated on a radical shift away from the hermeneutical principles that had governed the discussion of household order until the late medieval period. In light of Newman's insistence on the need for "continuity of principles," this kind of shift should lead to troublesome developments. It plunges us into strange debates about which models of political relations in the household are truly Christian. In some circles, this approach calls for a doctrinalization of patriarchal social order. The Council on Biblical Manhood and Womanhood insists that "biblical teaching" clearly asserts "the loving, humble leadership of redeemed husbands."[41] Others (e.g., Christians for Biblical Equality) press for a doctrinalization of more egalitarian models of family.[42] The claims of both Scripture and tradition, however, may be far more modest.

Perhaps the proponents of equal regard and its "biblicist" critics share a common error: the belief that Scripture must affirm one particular order of relations between the sexes — either egalitarian or hierarchical. Perhaps the theological quest for an ordained order of sexual relations is doomed. W. Shrage, Ruddolf Schnackenburg, and James Dunn argue that the Pauline and Pastoral *haustafeln* texts represent an exhortation to live under the Lordship of Christ within the institutions of the secular world.[43] The question of authority relations in marriage is essentially a political-ethical issue that is to be resolved by the culture, not a theological problematic for which Scripture provides a

---

40. Adrian von Speyr, *Letter to the Ephesians* (San Francisco: Ignatius, 1996), pp. 226-27.

41. "The Danvers Statement," *Christianity Today* (Jan. 13, 1989): 40-44.

42. Christians for Biblical Equality, "Men, Women, and Biblical Equality" (1989).

43. W. Shrage, "Sur Ethik der newtestamentlichen Haustafeln," *New Testament Studies* 21 (1974-75): 1-22.

textbook answer. Dunn and Schnackenburg note a "healthy worldli-
ness" in this approach.[44]

The New Testament codes lean on the best secular wisdom of
the time (Aristotelian political philosophy) in order to sort out basic
issues of household order. Scripture does raise a series of theological
concerns that bear upon the question of marital relationships: the
problem of indissolubility and divorce, the nature of the unity between husband and wife, the relationship between celibacy and marriage as distinct vocations. The politics of relations between the sexes
is not, however, a theological issue, and biblical authors are content
to lean on the common practice of their cultures in resolving this
question.

The consistent use of Aristotelian ethics to unpack the politics of
household relations suggests that this topic calls for a careful judgment of "practical reason" rather than a theological proclamation.
Considerations of justice, prudence, and equity do allow for very significant revisions, particularly when some of the key presuppositions that
informed traditional ethical judgments (for example, assumptions
about the "natural" inferiority of women) have been dismissed as untenable.

Conclusion

Catholicism is marked by a deep concern for the tradition of Christian
doctrinal teaching and the authentic development of this tradition.
Throughout the patristic and medieval periods questions of household
order and management were generally handled as a concern of political
ethics rather than a matter for theological speculation. Attempts to
doctrinalize this issue in late medieval Catholicism and Reformation
thought appear to be aberrant developments.

An implicit recognition of the nondoctrinal nature of this question may account for the flexible adjustment of the conservative Christian tradition to more egalitarian models of marriage in the modern
era. The Benedictine Monks of Solesmes collated over two hundred

---

44. See, for example, James D. G. Dunn, "The Household Rules in the New Testament," p. 50.

years of papal teaching on marriage from Benedict XIV to John XXIII.[45] Most of this material focuses upon the fundamental doctrinal dimensions of Catholic teaching on marriage and sexuality: sacramentality, indissolubility, consent, marital love, and the unitive and procreative dimensions of sexuality. References to headship and submission are briefly alluded to in just two documents: first, in a brief paragraph of Leo XIII's *Arcanum Divinae Sapientae* (1880), and again in a short section of Pius XI's encyclical on marriage, *Casti Connubii* (1930). Pius XI quotes Leo's discussion of Ephesians 5:21-33. He states that Ephesians 5 "implies" the "primacy of the husband." He immediately proceeds, however, to qualify this primacy: (1) this implied primacy cannot override the female's dignity and rights as a person, mother, and wife; (2) the wife is never to be treated on a level with minors; (3) her "submission" admits of degrees and varies according to historical circumstance; (4) if the husband neglects his functions she can shoulder his responsibilities without his consent. This very qualified discourse on the headship of the husband amounts to merely two pages in a six-hundred-page anthology on marriage.

Since the Second World War there is not any hint of the concept of one-sided conjugal subordination in the teaching of the Catholic church. A word search of the huge corpus of Vatican II documents and post-conciliar papal statements reveals only one reference to "headship and submission" language for conjugal relations — John Paul II's apostolic exhortation on the role and dignity of women, *Mulieris Dignitatem*. In this text the pope insists on mutual subordination in marriage and repudiates any "one-sided" theory of spousal subordination. He argues that the question of authority marks the point where the analogy between Christ/church and husband/wife breaks down: "whereas in the relationship between Christ and the Church the subjection is only on the part of the Church, in the relationship between husband and wife the 'subjection' is not one-sided but mutual."[46] The principle of "mutual subjection" in Christ represents the decisive "gospel innovation" for traditional patriarchal cultures, John Paul II emphasizes:

---

45. Benedictine Monks of Solesmes, eds., *Papal Teachings: Matrimony* (Boston: St. Paul's Editions, 1963).

46. John Paul II, *Mulieris Dignitatem*, no. 24.

The "innovation" of Christ is a fact: it constitutes the unambiguous content of the evangelical message and is the result of Redemption. However, the awareness that in marriage there is a mutual "subjection of the spouses out of reverence for Christ," and not just that of the wife to the husband, must gradually establish itself in the hearts, consciences, behaviour, and customs. This is a call which from that time onwards does not cease to challenge succeeding generations; it is a call which people have to accept ever anew. St. Paul not only wrote: "In Christ Jesus . . . there is no more man or woman," but also wrote: "there is no more slave or freeman." Yet how many generations were needed for such a principle to be realized in the history of humanity through the abolition of slavery! And what is one to say of the many forms of slavery to which individuals and peoples are subjected, which have not yet disappeared from history?[47]

Among some conservative Catholic voices, John Paul II's insistence on the principle of mutual subjection is dismissed as misleading, noninfallible theological opinion. There has never been, however, a tradition of formal doctrinal teaching endorsing subordination within the Catholic tradition. For much of the tradition the question of household order was treated as an issue of political ethics and theologians were content to follow the Pauline tradition of dependence on Aristotle's treatment of household order. In the modern period the issue was quietly shelved as church teaching focused on the covenantal nature of marital love. In the face of new moral perspectives on conjugal relations, John Paul II tells us that continued affirmation of one-sided subordination in marriage would be morally equivalent to employing Ephesians 5 as a Christian justification for the institution of slavery.

In light of this, there is little doubt that Newman would encourage us to embrace these developments and to press on, warning that "one cause of corruption in religion is the refusal to follow the course of doctrine as it moves on, and an obstinacy in the notions of the past."[48] Christianity may in some historical circumstances permit, but certainly does not teach, male headship in marriage.

47. John Paul II, *Mulieris Dignitatem*, no. 24.
48. John Henry Newman, *Essay on the Development of Christian Doctrine* (1878 ed.), p. 177.

CHAPTER II

Reflections on Headship

Maggie Gallagher

THE VIGOROUS differences outlined in these pages ought not obscure some basic agreement. As Mary Stewart Van Leeuwen points out, even among conservative evangelicals, belief in male headship "is not a confessional issue." Christians may legitimately disagree about such matters, either because the scriptural mandate is unclear or because, as several Catholic essayists herein point out, the most consistent line of scriptural interpretation tends to regard the question of male headship as a political or ethical issue, not a theological one. "The politics of household management deals with the natural order of social life," as Daniel Cere puts it.

Both the advocates of equal regard and at least its Catholic critics agree that interpretation of scriptural admonitions about male headship must be made in the larger context of the Christian teaching about marriage, in which themes of love, unity, mutality, and service are far more prominent. Good thing too, some women might say, since in the game of "text poker" the deck appears to the lay reader rather heavily stacked in favor of male headship. Compare and contrast the handful of biblical texts that Van Leeuwen identifies as traditionalist (Gen. 3:16, Eph. 5:22, 1 Cor. 11:3-10, and Tit. 2:5) with the egalitarian "factoids" (Gen. 1:26-28, Job 42:15, Acts 2:17-18, and Gal. 3:28), and the point becomes clear.

The distinguishing characteristic of the "traditionalist" hand in text poker is that all the verses speak rather directly and clearly to the issue of male headship. In Genesis, God tells Eve that as a consequence of her sin, "thy desire shall be to thy husband, and he shall rule over thee" (3:16).[1]

1. All biblical quotations in this essay are taken from the King James Version of the Bible.

Paul writes in Ephesians, "Wives, submit yourselves unto your own husbands, as unto the Lord. For the husband is the head of the wife, even as Christ is the head of the church. . . . Therefore, as the church is subject unto Christ, so let the wives be to their own husbands in everything" (5:22-24). In 1 Corinthians we read that "the head of every man is Christ; and the head of the woman is the man; and the head of Christ is God" (11:3). In Titus, Paul urges older women to teach young wives to be "discreet, chaste, keepers at home, good, obedient to their own husbands, that the word of God be not blasphemed" (2:5).

By contrast, the allegedly anti-headship scriptural verses do not seem particularly related to the issue of household management at all, even as they support the equality of women in a general sense. Genesis 1:27 clearly indicates that women too are made in the image of God ("in the image of God created he him; male and female created he them") and have dominion over fish and fowl and every living thing, but it is rather silent about the issue of family headship. (Both the corporation president and the factory worker are made in the image of God, but that doesn't mean the factory worker is not subordinate to the president for the purposes of work at least.) The news in Job 42:15, that Job gives his three fair daughters "inheritance among their brethren," seems even more obscurely related, as is the news in Acts 2:17 that both sons and daughters may receive the gift of prophecy. Galatians 3:28, which argues that in Christ "there is neither Jew nor Greek, there is neither bond nor free, there is neither male nor female: for ye are all one in Christ Jesus," is more to the point, radically marginalizing all social distinctions, which pale before the spiritual reality that faith in Jesus makes us all one. Still, such a marginalization can as easily be used to justify female subordination, since whether one is master or servant may be held to matter less in a world where what counts is the oneness we may have in Christ. What truly drives Christian thinking away from Aristotelian household codes toward mutuality in marriage is the latter half of Ephesians' admonitions:

> So ought men to love their wives as their own bodies. He that loveth his wife loveth himself. For no man ever yet hateth his own flesh; but nourisheth and cherisheth it, even as the Lord the church; For we are members of his body, of his flesh, and of his bones. For this cause shall a man leave his father and mother, and

shall be joined unto his wife, and they two shall be one flesh." (Eph. 5:28-31)

It is perhaps only a slight injustice to the intellectual richness of this debate to sum up the dialogue in these pages this way: conservative Protestants affirm male headship; liberal Protestants contest it; and Catholic thinkers stand on the sidelines saying, "headship-schmeadship — What really counts is indissolubility." Spend enough time pondering how two can become one, and (as Daniel Cere notes) you are drawn away, automatically, from discussions of household power relations. Headship is neither affirmed nor denied, in this way of interpreting Scripture, so much as simply put to one side.

That shift in language is part of the radical transformation Paul began when he talked in this unusual way (as Carolyn Osiek points out) of the husband as head of the wife, singular, rather than head of the family or other body, plural. "This is very rare outside the Pauline letters, possibly even unknown, and may suggest a different meaning," as Osiek puts it. The traditional analogy of power relations between, say, military commander and army breaks down immediately, radically, irrevocably, try as the early modern Catholic or Protestant reformers might to rebuild Ephesians from some practical advice about managing relationships into a message about divinely sanctioned female subordination.

Taking "one flesh" as literal truth, and not a metaphor, does make it hard to concentrate on issues of power relations, because the head is part of the body, and the body cannot be literally separated from its own head long enough to be subordinated. Even neighbor love seems inadequate to describe this relation: "Treat your stomach as you would like to be treated" hardly makes sense, does it? Try as they like, the Catholic thinkers cannot seem to address the topic head on; it keeps slipping away to the margins of the discussion. As, one might add, so often happens in the concrete experience of married life.

So it is perhaps not an accident, in this Catholic's view, that the very best question was asked by a Catholic woman, a friend of Carolyn Osiek who when asked about Christianity and male headship replied simply, "What is male headship?"

What is male headship? What function did it serve? Why is it that, for most of human history, families obviously required a head, and what is it about our present social organization that makes not just *male* headship but headship itself seem unnecessary in family life?

Following Aristotle's lead, most of these essays seem to accept that ancient civilizations conferred headship on males because of false cultural ideas about the inferiority of women. If this were the sole explanation for the existence of a family head then, as Cere notes, the whole idea is ripe for "significant revision" when, as now, "some of the key presuppositions that informed traditional ethical judgments (for example, assumptions about the 'natural' inferiority of women) have been dismissed as untenable."

Focusing exclusively on ancient ideas about gender misses something important: Aristotle, Paul, and just about everybody else for two thousand years assumed families needed heads for the same reason that we today unthinkingly accept the idea that corporations require heads. For most of human history, as Allan Carlson points out, families were the primary unit of production. Husband, wife, minor children, unmarried siblings, servants and apprentices, and aging adults depended on each other's labor for the food they ate and the clothes they wore. Coordinating the productive activities of diverse individuals was a critical necessity; the stakes could not be higher: if the family failed together to produce enough to eat, they would starve together. Then as now human beings could be stubborn, lazy, rebellious, shortsighted, selfish, and proud. Getting stiff-necked people to work together effectively and industriously for the common good (much less the glory of God) is always a difficult proposition, as the repeated letters of Paul to various early Christian communities make clear.

Hence the emphasis in the moral codes of all cultures (not just Greek and early Christian) on proper submission to family authority. The importance of this task was matched only by its human difficulty.

Today we often romanticize about the emotional joys of extended family living; in reality the experience of subordination to the needs of the extended family can be quite painful (and made more difficult by the fact that in many cases — because of high rates of death and remarriage — the subordination required is not just to one's own blood relatives but to one's in-laws and stepparents). In India's joint family system, for example, one key relationship seen as requiring subjection, and creating social anxiety about future household harmony, is not necessarily wife to husband but daughter-in-law to mother-in-law. Is the mother-in-law reasonable and considerate in her demands? Is the daughter-in-law willing to comply? If not, the peace and productivity of the household is in jeopardy.

And families, of course, though they have the advantage of "kin altruism" and strong emotional ties, must make do without the set of market incentives corporate presidents routinely use to get employees to submit to one another: family members cannot (in traditional societies at least) be fired, nor will they be paid more or less in accordance with their contributions. Greater productivity translates into collective rewards, not personal ones. The purpose of household codes in all cultures, with their emphasis on submission, was, it seems to me, to reduce the "transaction costs" that would threaten the very viability of the household if family members felt free to engage in extended periods of intersubjective dialogue in order to decide (like the friends of the Little Red Hen) who was to plant the seed, or harvest the wheat, or bake the bread.

Today we imagine families as being less like little factories and more like, say, book clubs — places where like-minded, affectionate people gather to exchange ideas, share feelings, and seek companionship and personal identity, a sense of belonging. A book club can get along without a head, because nothing immediately consequential in the world happens if decisions are not made: the group can intersubjectively dialogue to its heart's content until a consensus emerges or the cows come home and no harm to any of the members will result. Indeed, they may even enjoy it, which is the point of the association in the first place.

One, if not the main, reason male headship has come under challenge, then, if I am right is not new scientific or cultural discoveries about equality between the sexes but dramatic changes in the economic means of production; family members depend upon the market, rather than each other, to supply the family's collective needs.

One challenge to standard feminist discourse about the family, then, becomes this: why is it that submission to husbands is now almost universally regarded as degrading to women while submission to corporate presidents is not? The dirty little secret the men in gray flannel suits hid from their fifties' housewives is that work requires subordination and conformity as well as creativity and reward: the move to market roles involves an immense submission of time, energy, and mission to a hierarchy much larger, more impersonal, and perhaps even more morally demanding than the family — for productive and successful workers are those who make the goals of the corporation their own, and increasingly, as the world shrinks, on a twenty-four–seven basis.

At the same time, the degree of submission family requires has been drastically circumscribed. What does male headship mean in a contemporary context, now that it no longer means deciding which field to plant, or what cow to sell, if the family is to survive? What advocates of equal regard denounce under the scary label "soft patriarchy" seems to many women who've experienced it, I suspect, an extremely negligible price to pay for male support and cooperation in family life. Men who wish to abuse, terrorize, and control their wives certainly cannot look to Scripture for justification. (Nor, I suspect, do they; the latest research shows that cohabitors are more likely than spouses to commit domestic violence, which throws cold water on the idea that male domestic terrorism is rooted in traditional ideas about marital roles.[2]) Indeed, to this lay reader one thing is clear from Ephesians: Scripture gives men no right to "stand on their rights" in relation to their wives, to enforce wives' submission by so much as an angry word. The overwhelming message of these passages — suffer little wrongs patiently, for Christ's sake — certainly applies to men and women equally.

What do we mean these days by suggesting that the husband is head of the family? "One meaning it does not have," reports Robert Weiss in his study of the inner lives of successful men, "is that he is the family's boss." When Weiss asked students and workshop attendees to role-play a family meeting about a vacation, for example, something interesting happened: Almost always "the woman playing the mother has taken the lead. She has asked the husband for his ideas, has elicited reactions from the children, has made her own suggestions and has piloted the way to compromise." The man is told he is an avid fisherman and the woman is told she does not want to spend her vacations with the kids cleaning fish. "Sometimes the man held out stubbornly for the trout stream, but always the woman won him around." Although she exercises her power diplomatically, notes Weiss, "the woman would be

2. Linda J. Waite and Maggie Gallagher, *The Case for Marriage* (New York: Doubleday, 2000).

the marital partner who was really running things in the family." Once a decision was made, however, notes Weiss, "The man would turn to me and nod, to indicate that the family had come to a resolution. Though the woman had piloted the resolution, the man would assume responsibility for presenting it to me." In sum, reports Weiss, "In family life, the man is not head of the family in the sense he gets his way; often enough he ends by endorsing his wife's plans. He is family head in that he represents the family in its dealings with the world."[3] Especially, one might add, the world of other men.

The reality Weiss observes in these long-married executive husbands is that male headship in families is largely an honorific title. It is a title that reconciles men to the loss of their freedom — including the freedom to flee — while at the same time culturally affirming what biology has not made obvious to men: their importance in the drama of creating new life. Male headship is grounded in the same biosocial reality that explains why even the most committed feminist (in my own limited experience), intent on keeping her own name and identity within marriage, usually confers her husband's name on the children.[4] This is an act of female generosity, a recognition of the superiority that in this way at least female biology confers. The mother knows the children of her body. By giving the children the father's name, the male, the mother, and society attempt to make up for what biology has not given the man: an obvious, visible relationship to his own children.

When men mistake headship for bossdom, when men do not find a way to graciously bow to a wife's expressed needs and desires, divorce is the likely result.[5] Or young men, correctly perceiving that marriage increases female power over them, may refuse to marry at all. In inner-city neighborhoods, reports Elijah Anderson, "In a great number of cases, peer group or no, the boy will send the girl on her way even if she is carrying a baby he knows is his. . . . He . . . does not want to put up with married life, which he sees as giving a woman some say in how he spends his time." For these young men, "It is much easier and more fun

3. Robert S. Weiss, *Staying the Course: The Emotional and Social Lives of Men Who Do Well At Work* (New York: Free Press, 1990), pp. 126-27.

4. My thanks to David Blankenhorn for this analogy, not to be confused with an endorsement of my argument.

5. John M. Gottman et al., "Predicting Marital Happiness and Stability from Newlywed Interactions," *Journal of Marriage and the Family* 60, no. 1 (February 1998): 5, 18.

to stay home and 'take care of Mama,' some say; when taking care consists of 'giving her some change for room and board,' eating good food, and being able 'to come as I want and to go as I please.'"[6]

The experience of married life for men is of submission to the female domain: of attachment, order, love, babies — a life lived in the service of others, a daily round of duty, no glorious last stands. The uncivilized male virtues must be radically transformed if not jettisoned, if men are to perform as husbands and fathers. In communities where the roles of husbands and fathers are culturally marginalized, these uncivilized masculine virtues reappear with shocking suddenness.

How do we get men to submit to female domain, if not dominion? The whole point of headship language is that it is a strategy for obtaining male submission to the terms of family life, to the woman's point of view of the relative place of wilding, male bonding, retaliation, outlawing, and even the more mundane "coming and going as I please" in the large scheme of life.

In its most basic form, male headship offers men an excuse to submit to the demands of family life — and to the reality that wives retain considerable power, control, and authority in the home over the daily life of the husband. "I make all the big decisions and she makes the little ones," a husband of this sort is apt to remark: "Funny how in forty-five years, no big decisions have come up yet." Traditionally the wife (who may or may not also work outside the home) decides what the family eats, what it wears, often where it lives (deciding what school district or community is appropriate for the children, for example), where it vacations, what kind of childcare is adequate (parental, relatives, nanny, or day care center), and what the daily household routines will be. "And so far as our social schedule, she probably takes care of that in the sense of what we're going to be doing on Friday night or Wednesday or Sunday," reports one businessman. In matters of discipline and pedagogy, her theories reign supreme. "I tend to go along with the wife's beliefs and desires in terms of what the kids should have and what would be good for them," says another executive.[7] She may consult extensively with her husband, but because she is more often

---

6. Elijah Anderson, *The Code of the Street: Decency, Violence, and the Moral Life of the Inner City* (New York: Norton, 1999), pp. 173-75.

7. Quoted in Weiss, *Staying the Course,* pp. 124-26.

the one who implements each of these decisions, he has little power to contravene her determined choice. In many cases, a man loses effective control over his entire paycheck, as well as his leisure, when he chooses marriage.[8] Dependence is a double-edged sword. For every wife who depends on her husband for the majority of the family income, there is a husband who depends on his wife to give him a home and a family and even a raison d'etre.

Yet inside of marriage, men surrender this degree of power willingly, without a sense of subordination. When the marriage dissolves, you can see the process unravel, as a new male discourse of injustice arises when men suddenly realize how little control they have over their children's daily lives. Both feminists and fathers' advocates have noted the same basic dynamic: Delegating this power to an ex-wife — a non-family member — threatens males' sense of connection with their own children. Sanford Braver, a scholar and advocate for divorced fathers, captured this dynamic in a nutshell reporting on interviews with a sample of divorcing fathers in Maricopa County, Arizona: "Many of the fathers interviewed felt that everything about the divorce, especially anything concerning the way the children were raised, was completely out of their control. They felt as if the child was in no real sense *theirs* any more. The child, in effect, belonged now to someone else, someone who, not uncommonly, despised and disparaged them."[9]

"Hurt feelings were compounded by resentments about a former wife's evident discretionary authority in divorce; much of women's power is kept hidden in marriage," writes feminist scholar Terry Arendell in her study of divorced men; "the shift, in which she apparently gained authority, was a direct affront to assumptions about the sexes and their relationships." Even husbands who aren't affronted can be disconcerted by the difference between delegating primary care-taking to a spouse and an ex-spouse: "I can't say I didn't want the divorce; it was a mutual decision. I wanted my freedom," one ex-husband

8. "Married men may do about one hour a week less in housework than cohabiting men, but they spend significantly more time in the labor market than single men and they also experience large drops in leisure time, compared to singles. Married men not only have less leisure, they are more likely to spend leisure time with their wives, doing things 'as a family'" (Waite and Gallagher, *The Case for Marriage*).

9. Sanford L. Braver, *Divorced Dads: Shattering the Myths* (New York: Jeremy P. Tarcher/Putnam, 1999).

told Arendell; "the freedom is a great benefit, *great.* But I just hadn't understood before what it would do. It's really become them and me, and I don't know what to do."[10]

Male headship within the family need not be grounded in female inferiority, in what Van Leeuwen describes as the "kind of essentialism that says that men, either naturally or by divine fiat, are to be 'aggressive' (or at least more assertive) and women are to be 'passive' (or at least much less assertive)." Once we take the family seriously as an important arena of life, we can recognize that the need for a culturally created male role in the family is grounded in female natural superiority in this arena — in the reality that all women are connected to their children from birth in a way that the male need not be and seldom will be, without the enthusiastic support and encouragement of the mother.

The advocates of equal regard, it seems to me, have not yet fully explored the implications of their own rhetorical advance — that truly equal regard between men and women must include a radical revaluation of traditional women's work. Have we incorporated too many masculinist assumptions into our own conception of demeaning gender roles within the family? The genius of the language of equal regard is that it points away, simultaneously, from *both* androgynous and patriarchal (or masculinist) conceptions of family life. Husbands and wives, it suggests, don't have to fulfill exactly the same functions in order to be equal partners. Nor can the work women do in creating families and building neighborhoods and communities any longer be seen (as it was often portrayed in the fifties) as a service they perform for their husbands, to free the men up for the more important, demanding, "real" work of conquering continents or climbing corporate hierarchies.

While equal-regard advocates in this book are willing to permit men and women to adopt different functions, they are unwilling to allow culture or religion to attach social meanings to gender. At times they seem to argue that Christian ideals of mutuality and neighbor love at a minimum imply, if they do not command, that Christians ought to reject all but the most minimal sexual scripts. Roles must remain conceptually androgynous, fluid, the subject of intersubjective dialogue, if women and men are to be "free." The attempt to define any

10. Terry Arendell, *Fathers and Divorce* (Thousand Oaks: Sage, 1995), pp. 58-65.

gender role at all within the family, not just the idea of male headship, is in their view a violation of equal regard, and of the commandment to neighbor love. For example, Don Browning makes this critique of the "servant headship" model of the male role in the family: "They seem to suggest that a little soft patriarchy is the price to be paid for male responsibility," Browning chides; "I agree that there is something important in the idea of male servanthood, but not necessarily in male servant headship. I recommend following Paul's belief that servanthood should apply to both wives and husbands."

While equal-regard advocates permit in theory husbands and wives to do different things within a marriage, they retreat at the idea that one's sex should influence these decisions. Husbands may have a servant role in the family, but not really a male role. Equal-regard language flirts with the idea that gender may be important to family life, but equal-regard advocates beat a swift retreat at any practical incarnation of this idea. "Moreover, establishing and maintaining the full equality between husband and wife requires an awareness and constant renegotiation of the often uneven distribution of private and public responsibilities and power between husband and wife," writes Bonnie Miller-McLemore. As she describes it, "roles and duties in parenting and sexuality are social and physical arrangements women and men must constantly renegotiate. . . . Gender stereotypes signal an onerous breakdown in this process with negative consequences for all involved."

Difference between husband and wife in family life need not be rooted in ideas of female inferiority; indeed, equal regard may ask women to recognize that gendered meanings in the family spring from female superiority, or at least uniquely feminine powers. Women, it is becoming increasingly clear, permit the creation of fathers. (Even God, it might be noted, looked for Mary's assent.) Women make babies but they also make fathers and families. Everywhere in the mammalian world, sociobiologists note, the tie between mother and child is much less fragile than that between father and child. In human terms the claims of the father must be made through the mother, with her assent, through marriage or some other means. When mothers no longer actively support or encourage the fatherhood of men, when the assent of the mother is withdrawn, as often happens in divorce, the practical result in most cases will be the eventual end of fatherhood. One man interviewed by Terry Arendell compared the fate of his fatherhood in two different divorces: "Anyway, even after my first divorce, I found that my ex-wife was vital to my relationship with the child of our marriage: She thought it was important that he maintain contact with me and that I be a part of his life. So she really encouraged him to do this and so it continued to be a relationship. She ran a kind of interference between us. He's 21 now, and we have a good, solid relationship, but my children of this last marriage are essentially withdrawn from me. Their mother, my second wife, never really facilitated our relationship."[11]

Even when mothers are willing, the ability of men to father when placed outside the charmed circle of the mother-child family is, well, problematic. When the claims of mothers and fathers on their children come into conflict, fathers typically lose, perhaps especially now that family life is increasingly grounded in emotional rather than economic ties.

The genius of John Miller's contribution to this volume is that he has come up with a scriptural answer to the male problematic that is not rooted in Ephesians 5, an answer to the ticklish issue of power struggles between men and women in our changing social context. Instead he asks men to look to the fatherhood of God to learn how to ground a male role in the family in a way that is true, attractive to men, and acceptable to women made understandably skittish by language of headship. Miller poses a challenge to Browning (and other equal-regard advocates who understand the male problematic) that seems to me unanswered, at least in this volume:

> It would be better, [Browning] implies, if the ideal of "male servant headship" would be redefined as "servanthood," located "as a moment . . . within love as mutuality," and then applied equally to husbands and wives. But is this redefined teaching what wives actually need if "male ambivalence to fatherhood" is to be addressed? Can such a generalized and degendered teaching still speak to the male problematic? Browning . . . acknowledges the inadequacies of a marital ethic of equal regard for dealing with the male problematic and concedes that New Testament headship teaching does effectively address this issue. *What he does not show is how this New Testament teaching remains effective when stripped of its specificity for men and redefined as he proposes.*

11. Quoted in Arendell, *Fathers and Divorce*, p. 63.

Children need fathers who love them and provide for them. Women need husbands who are affectionate, reliable, helpful, protective, and responsive. How do we create such men? Under what sort of conditions are new fathers and better husbands likely to proliferate?

Equal-regard advocates place a big bet on getting men (and women) to adopt a new, more egalitarian and less sacrificial marriage ethic. But when it comes to creating involved fathers (and relieving the burdens of working mothers) there is some indication that attachment to a masculine role in the family is far more key than fostering egalitarian gender roles.[12] In one recent study of parents and preschool-aged children, "gender role attitudes were not related to paternal involvement in child-care tasks" including feeding, bathing, dressing, meal attendance, or one-on-one activities. When it came to older, school-aged children, gender role traditionalism in fathers reduced one-on-one activities but actually increased fathers' involvement in youth activities (coaching, PTA, church groups, etc.).[13]

Even feminist scholars are beginning to recognize that money and power won in the market can give women freedom from relationships but not the power to create loving interdependence. One recent study of equally shared parenting, for example, concluded that

> Compared to the unequal women, equally sharing mothers may simply possess more power in their relationships because they are relatively less attached to their husbands than their husbands are to them, or because compared to other men, their husbands care more about having children and their relationships with children. . . . Interestingly, by and large, the power equally sharing women report using is not economic power. Their power is derived

12. Note that Arlie Hochschild found that apart from a small number of highly committed egalitarians, the men who did the most housework and childcare were not the moderately egalitarian men but the traditional "family men." One suspects this is because these were men who located their status as men in their roles as husbands and fathers rather than in climbing status hierarchies in the workplace. (Arlie Russell Hochschild, with Anne Machung, *The Second Shift: Working Parents and the Revolution at Home* [New York: Viking, 1989].)

13. W. Bradford Wilcox, "Emerging Attitudes about Gender Roles and Fatherhood," in *The Faith Factor in Fatherhood*, ed. Don E. Eberly (Lanham, Md.: Lexington Books, 1999).

from their husbands' love for them and their husbands' desire to have children.[14]

Women in families have power when men long to be husbands and fathers. Men who are attached to their roles as husband and father find inevitably that they must come to terms with the needs, desires, and power of the woman by whom and through whom these valued titles are conferred. As Kierkegaard put it,

> Through her I am Man, for only a married man is an authentic man; compared with this any other title is nothing and actually presupposes this. Through her I am Father — any other position of honor is but a human invention, a fad that is forgotten in a hundred years. Through her I am Head of the Family; through her I am Defender of the Home, Breadwinner, Guardian of the Children.[15]

Men to whom such titles do not carry intense personal and sexual meaning, by contrast, leave women with little power in the marital relationship. Women who must beg husbands to have children have less power than wives whose husbands are happily expecting the event. Perhaps the worst of all worlds when it comes to power in marriage is experienced by wives married to men with minimal commitment to being husbands. Sociologist Karla Hackstaff describes such an unattractive combination of what she called "male dominance" and "divorce culture" in her book *Marriage in a Culture of Divorce*: "I've told my wife she better do as I say, or I'll divorce her and she'll find herself in the poor house." Another husband threatened to divorce his wife if she did not let him remain "the boss." By contrast, even within traditional couples, male commitment to marital permanence "set ideological limits on the power of the husband."[16]

What is the male role in families? Why do families need men? If "equal regard" is to achieve its stated aim — to come up with truer,

14. Francine M. Deutsch, *Halving it All: How Equally Shared Parenting Works* (Cambridge, Mass.: Harvard University Press, 1999), pp. 65-66.

15. Søren Kierkegaard, "Some Reflections on Marriage," in *Wing to Wing, Oar to Oar: Readings on Courting and Marrying*, ed. Amy A. Kass and Leon R. Kass (Notre Dame, Ind.: University of Notre Dame Press, 2000), p. 123.

16. Karla B. Hackstaff, *Marriage in a Culture of Divorce* (Philadelphia: Temple University Press, 1999), pp. 75-87.

more Christian, and more satisfying answers to the male problematic — it must come up with answers to questions like these, essentially gendered questions that imply gendered answers. Equal regard is an attractive ethic in its own right, but not an answer to the problem of males' lesser attachment to and place within the natural family. A call to intersubjective dialogue is indeed a rigorous ethic, and not one likely to bring males back in flocks. Indeed, if women understand men's roles in this way it is likely to increase women's discontent, to reinforce the already prevalent idea that men are simply being willfully obstinate and unfair in not displaying more of the traditionally feminine virtues in family life.

Equal regard authorizes a new understanding of male and female roles within the family that is not based upon the subordination of women. Difference need not imply subordinate. This is its potential genius. But because its authors remain trapped in "soft androgyny," they are as yet unable to exploit what I believe may be a vitally important conceptual advance in describing and creating equality in families.

Reflections on the Debate

Don Browning

IN RESPONDING to the critics of "equal regard," I will first address the important comments and criticisms of Allan Carlson and John Miller and then conclude with responses to the several interesting points of Robert Godfrey, Daniel Cere, and Maggie Gallagher.

Allan Carlson, John Miller, and the authors of *From Culture Wars to Common Ground* agree on several important issues. We agree that male responsibility as husband and father is fragile. We agree that Christianity developed powerful religio-cultural symbols and truths that worked to counteract male reluctance to bond with wife and children. But both Carlson and Miller believe male responsibility requires male headship. On this, we disagree.

On behalf of the members of our project who contributed to this volume, I thank both Carlson and Miller for their thoughtful essays. Both raise important questions. In every case, however, I think we can answer these questions and, in so doing, advance our case. Our purpose is not, however, to win the argument but, instead, to develop a broad ecumenical theological and practical strategy to strengthen families in our time — one that would incorporate many insights from Carlson and Miller.

Carlson and the Yeoman Farm Family

Allan Carlson and I are members of the Council on Families in America. We have worked on and signed several papers released by this council, most notably *Marriage in America: A Report to the Nation.*[1] We agree on many issues, even though our cultural and theological positions differ. Carlson concentrates primarily on *From Culture Wars to Common Ground* in his essay and advances several objections.

To begin with, Carlson charges us with building a family ethic of equal regard by creating our own biblical canon and emphasizing some texts at the exclusion of others. But this can hardly be true since we discuss the Gospels, the pre-Pauline and Pauline texts, and the Pastoral Epistles. It is more likely that Carlson simply has a different interpretation of such texts. Take Ephesians 5:21-33. Most theological liberals completely skip that text because it is so often employed to defend male headship. We, however, use it and show that when interpreted in context, Ephesians modifies, although never completely dismantles, the systematic patriarchy of Aristotle — the principal source of the family ideology in urban centers surrounding early Christianity.

Ephesians was embedded in Aristotelian patriarchy yet reacted against it. Hence, in reacting against the Aristotelian codes, it commanded couples to "be subject to one another," husbands to love wives as "Christ loved the church," and husbands to love their wives "as they do their own bodies" — all quite at odds with Aristotle's aristocratic paternalism. Ephesians did retain the codes sufficiently to instruct wives to be subject to their husbands, but given all the changes it made in the Aristotelian codes, it is clear that the direction of Ephesians was away from the Aristotelian model and toward a love ethic of equal regard. In advancing a theological interpretation that completes this direction, we are simply following the interpretive rule set down by Jesus when he said, "on these two commandments [to love God and neighbor] hang all the law and the prophets" (Matt. 22:40). Time and again, the New Testament makes neighbor love the interpretive center of its ethic (see, for example, Matt. 19:19; 22:39; Mark 12:31-33; Luke 10:27; Gal. 5:14; James 2:8).

Against the background of the honor-shame codes of the Greco-Roman world, Ephesians, and much of the New Testament, takes a giant step toward bringing neighbor love directly into the family, something Carlson will not do. In contrast, we believe that our overall theological obligation is not the narrow task of interpreting a text in isola-

---

1. *Marriage in America: A Report to the Nation* (New York: Institute for American Values, 1995).

tion from the entire gospel but to understand it in light of Jesus' wider teachings. This is not the creation of a new canon, as Carlson charges; it is a matter of theological interpretation analogous to the step Luther took in rendering the gospel in light of the central theme of justification by faith.

Carlson agrees with us that Ephesians helps overcome male reluctance to bond with wife and child. He insists, however, that male responsibility requires soft patriarchy where the husband "holding headship . . . is charged with self-renouncing sacrifice" for the wife's well-being. Sounds good. Indeed, it is very close to our position. We join Carlson in emphasizing early Christianity's ingenious call for husbands and fathers to identify with the sacrificial and steadfast love of Christ. But Carlson interprets this to mean that the husband should make the decisions about what is good for the wife. Along with the Promise Keepers, he does not understand the intersubjective nature of neighbor love as applied to spouses. To know what is good for the other, one must create through dialogue a shared understanding of that good. Carlson retains the idea that male responsibility entails male executive prerogative and imagines that this is the teaching of Jesus and the gospel. The husband must be sacrificial; here we agree. But must he also be Aristotle's aristocratic head who uses his power for the good of his wife? On this point, I think that Carlson is far closer to the traditions of Athens than he is to the gospel.

Hence, we do not devalue Christian love. We simply have a different view of it than Carlson. Our view of Christian love as equal regard or mutuality follows the strict demands of Christian neighbor love; we must love our wife or husband with the same seriousness that we love ourselves. But our spouses too are to love us with the same seriousness that they love themselves. This formulation of love is especially important for women and minorities who are often asked to endure exploitation in the name of sacrificial love. Nevertheless, there is a place for sacrificial love within a love ethic of equal regard, and we explain this at length in our book. Since we live in a world of sin and brokenness, Christians are called to the self-sacrifice of the cross, not as an end in itself but as means for restoring broken relations to a condition of mutuality. This view of Christian love puts sacrificial love in its proper context as a necessary step toward restoring mutuality. Sacrificial love need not require headship.

In the history of Christian thought, there are competing interpretations of Christian love. Although the authors of *From Culture Wars to Common Ground* are Protestants, we gravitate to an understanding of Christian love as mutuality or equal regard that is closer to some Catholic views. According to Anders Nygren in his great *Agape and Eros,* some significant Protestant views have made self-sacrifice an end in itself.[2] In other cases, sacrificial love can be a camouflage for making decisions for others, as it may be for Carlson.

Carlson goes on to ask why, if love as equal regard is so good, are the liberal denominations that hold this view also the ones that are declining. But certainly Carlson would agree that denominational growth itself is no criterion of spiritual truth. More to the point, however, our answer would be this: the ethic of equal regard needs to be energized and surrounded by the narrative of Christ's self-sacrificial love. This we strongly and repeatedly assert. Some liberal denominations may have lost sight of this additional truth. Furthermore, they may have become too general in their use of this ethic and may have lost an understanding of its relevance to parenthood, the two-parent family, and the concreteness of marriage.

Carlson fears that the love ethic of equal regard will result in endless calculation and bargaining between husband and wife, but here Carlson simply misinterprets the meaning of the concept. Love as equal regard is not what Kant called the "hypothetical imperative" (i.e., if you do this for me, I will return the favor to you). Both other and self in the ethic of equal regard are treated as persons deserving unconditioned respect and goodwill. Within this framework, both husband and wife are to do good to the other, work for the welfare of the other, and contribute to the other's health, comfort, and growth. Negotiations about respective roles and goods must occur within this deeper unconditioned respect. Negotiating about specific goods and rights must not in the ethic of equal regard trump mutual respect and goodwill.

And yes, contra Carlson, phrases such as "a covenant of intersubjective dialogue" as an elaboration of the meaning of equal regard do enrich our understanding of the "one flesh" relation between husband and wife. Without such qualifications, the idea of one flesh can

2. Anders Nygren, *Agape and Eros* (Philadelphia: Westminster, 1953).

be interpreted to mean that the identities of both parties disappear into some new undifferentiated oneness. But loving neighbor or spouse as oneself requires no such obliteration of selves.

Carlson believes that *From Culture Wars to Common Ground* neglects to account for the impact of industrialization on families. It also disregards, he contends, the long struggle by the labor movement to receive an adequate family wage. In saying this, he ignores our discussion in chapter 2 of the impact of technical rationality and market economies on families, the whole of chapter 3 which amplifies this, the discussion in chapter 8 of Pope Leo XIII's *Rerum Novarum* and his defense of the family wage, and finally our host of recommendations addressing work and family issues in the eleventh chapter. Carlson himself has been an advocate of larger tax deductions and credits for families with children; we advocate these measures as well. Moreover, he overlooks our central practical proposal, a radical remaking of society so that couples with children would work in the wage economy between them no more than sixty hours a week. (This might be divided thirty-thirty or forty-twenty.) This proposal leaves time for parenting and attention to each other.

Despite all this, we should not, as I think Carlson does, overemphasize the differences between our two positions. We both believe that there is a male problematic, that the New Testament brilliantly balances it, and that there is a strong role for self-sacrifice in any adequate Christian family ethic. And we concur that modern market economies must be drastically restructured to be family friendly. These and other agreements make Carlson an important dialogue partner for the Religion, Culture, and Family Project.

Miller: Does Male Responsibility Really Require Male Headship?

The areas of agreement between John Miller and our project are massive. Had he concentrated on *From Culture Wars to Common Ground* in addition to the essays in this volume and other project writings, the agreements might be even more pronounced. Miller agrees with us that the absence of fathers from families is a major issue for our time, that male commitment to families is generally tentative, and that Judaism and early Christianity made major contributions to developing a new model of fatherhood.

But Miller believes, as does Carlson, that male headship is a prerequisite for male responsibility. As far as I can tell, he advances neither biblical nor theological justifications for this stand. It simply seems to be very difficult for him to separate headship and responsibility. All scholars of the Bible realize that there is plurality and tension between different scriptural passages and that diverse notes and tones are struck in the various texts. The task is to find what is fundamental and pervasive and use this to unify the differing emphases. Miller recognizes this task but concludes that headship is one of these integrating themes and crucial to male responsibility. In doing this, he disregards the centrality of neighbor love and its implications for a love ethic of equal regard.

Miller is clearly attracted to our concept of the "male problematic." He appears to accept our use of evolutionary psychology to show how most male mammals do not bond with children and consort and why human males probably also retain tendencies not to do so. Miller thinks, however, that we give no adequate answer to the very problem we posed; it seems to me that he fails to understand the answer we have given.

Even in the material Miller has read, he overlooks our strong emphasis on the Christian man's identification with the sacrificial love of Christ. In my essay in this book, I pointed out that Thomas Aquinas interpreted the "Ephesians analogy between Christ's sacrificial love for the church and a husband's love for his family as having the clear intent of stabilizing male hesitancy to bond." And in *From Culture Wars to Common Ground*, we argued that this recapitulation by Christian men of God's sacrificial love follows what historians of religion believe is the very essence of our experience of the sacred. The Christian man's identification with the sacrifice of Christ is crucial to our argument. Miller, like Carlson, seems to overlook this.

Both Miller and Carlson believe that because we hold equal regard to be central to a Christian marriage ethic, we must not mean what we say about the role of self-sacrifice in Christian love. But we do mean it. We simply locate self-sacrifice as a moment within the larger strenuous ethic of mutuality and equal regard. Christ's sacrifice is aimed at restoring an unbroken relation with humans; Christian husbands and wives exhibit sacrificial love, not as an end in itself, but as a means of restoring loving relations of equal regard and mutuality.

Finally, the sacrificial commitment required of the Christian man builds on, yet redirects, natural human tendencies. Our discussion of the role of human infant dependence, paternal certainty, kin altruism, sexual exchange, and mutual helpfulness is not to say that any of these conditions, or all together, are sufficient to secure male bonding and responsibility. We discuss them because Aquinas had the profound insight that the commitments of equal regard and self-sacrifice have some natural inclinations to build on, even as they redirect them. The natural arguments for male investment are important because many people in our society have forgotten them. And, of course, to talk about the natural tendencies behind the male problematic is not to exclude sin; it shows instead that sin can further distort our conflicting natural tendencies just as grace can channel them toward more morally productive directions.

Once again, I thank Allan Carlson and John Miller for their thoughtful responses to our work and hope that this and other exchanges will go far toward building a new marriage culture for America, one to which Christians will make, as they have in the past, decisive contributions.

Godfrey, Cere, and Gallagher

I will conclude with comments on Godfrey, Cere, and Gallagher. First, some remarks about Robert Godfrey's review of the biblical evidence for male headship. When reading his remarks, I was struck by his extensive summary of the many ways in which both Old and New Testaments portray such a wide range of male-female equality — spiritual equality before God, equality in redemptive work, and equal responsibility for sin. The authors of *From Culture Wars to Common Ground* certainly agree with his excellent review of the relevant scriptural passages. Nonetheless, Godfrey insists that both Old and New Testaments explicitly teach male headship. We claim, on the other hand, that both parts of the Bible *assume* the pervasive patriarchy of all ancient societies but that the Jesus movement, pre-Pauline Christianity, and elements of Pauline Christianity subtly undermined classical patriarchy.

My major complaint about Godfrey's argument centers on what is also strong about his presentation: he knows the biblical texts very well — too well. He puts nothing in context, makes no effort to interpret passages in light of knowledge about surrounding social and cultural traditions, and handles every text as if it were of equal importance to the central message of Christianity. First, context. Certainly he is partially correct; the seeds of some headship themes in the New Testament have origins in the Old Testament. But are we to absolutize ancient androcentrism and assume that to understand Old Testament theology we must also retain the patriarchy of ancient societies of the Mediterranean areas, including the patriarchy of ancient Israel? And is it really true that we have no evidence, as Godfrey charges, for the decisive role of the Aristotelian tradition on the relation of family to polis in early Christianity? I mentioned in chapter 1 of this volume the seminal work on the origin of the household codes by David Balch in his analysis of 1 Peter[3] and the Osiek/Balch book *Families in the New Testament World*.[4] Godfrey gives no indication that he consulted these works. To focus our argument once again, let me say this: our point is that the Aristotelian pattern provides the *systematic* threefold framework (husbands and wives, fathers and children, masters and slaves) for the patriarchal household codes in the New Testament. This is true for the simple reason that Roman Hellenism had bequeathed them to the urban centers of the Mediterranean world. These codes pervaded the atmosphere of those societies like the desert breeze. But early Christianity — especially Ephesians 5:21-33 — put a new and creative twist on that legacy, a truth that conservative Christian scholars such as Robert Godfrey should come clean on, acknowledge, and convey to the lay people they influence.

In Godfrey's view of biblical interpretation, there is no distinction in the Old Testament between the Priestly materials and the Jahwist materials and no distinction in the New Testament between the possible words of Jesus, Paul, Q, or pre-Q. There is no positioning of the social and cultural contexts of texts and no discussion of what knowledge

---

3. David Balch, *Let Wives Be Submissive: The Domestic Code in 1 Peter* (Atlanta: Scholars Press, 1981).

4. Carolyn Osiek and David Balch, *Families in the New Testament World: Households and House Churches* (Louisville: Westminster/John Knox, 1997).

about such things adds to the proper interpretation of Scripture. There is for him no theological core from which less central texts are measured — nothing like Luther's justification by faith, Barth's Word of God, or Jesus' own affirmation of the Great Commandment as the summary of the Law. All texts have the same authority — from Genesis to 1 Timothy, from Joel to Revelation. The unity of the Bible for Godfrey is so profound, so unambiguous, so transparent that there are no theological decisions to make, no interpretive issues that need balancing, no problems in separating gospel from culture. Nor are there challenges in distinguishing the pastoral and agrarian ways of Semitic tribes from the abiding views of Jesus, Paul, and their great interpreters such as Augustine, Aquinas, and Luther. In the end, Godfrey and the authors of *From Culture Wars to Common Ground* disagree on the appropriateness of a theology of equal regard for marriage and families because we have profoundly different views of the Bible and its relation to theology.

Our view of the relation of biblical interpretation and theology is much closer to Daniel Cere's careful discussion of John Henry Newman's "continuity of principle." Cere is correct in distinguishing doctrine from the political anthropology carried by ancient cultures and sometimes used by Christian thinkers to articulate theologies of family and marriage. This is the distinction that Godfrey is unable to make, even to recognize. His failure to understand the difference leads him to "doctrinalize" (to use a concept from Cere) the ancient political anthropology of patriarchy.

Although I can commend Cere's essay almost without reservation, I do have one slight concern about his argument. I wonder if he does not separate doctrine and political anthropology too decisively? He is correct, and instructive, in showing how aristocratic Aristotelian patriarchy continued in the family theologies of both Augustine and Aquinas. He is also right in holding that Augustine and Aquinas were far more interested in other aspects of their family theologies than in their lingering paternalism. But he may fail to fully credit how theological ideas, such as the image of God in humans (the *imago Dei*) have implications for gender relations that sooner or later realize in history their inner logic and lead us to credit full equality in all respects to women, both inside and outside of families and marriage. It is true that Aquinas was more interested in stating the theological grounds for the indissolubility of marriage than he was in giving a theological justification for male headship. But today, our concern with marital permanence cannot be stated so strongly as to eclipse the philosophical and theological grounds for the equal-regard marriage.

Finally, I must answer some of the important points in Maggie Gallagher's engaging essay. Gallagher has sympathies with the idea of the equal-regard marriage but fears that appeals to equality alone are insufficient to keep husbands and fathers integrated with the fundamental family matrix of mother and child. The truth is, we are concerned about that as well, and we directly address these issues in ways Gallagher has missed. Some of our arguments dealing with these concerns are in my essay in this book and some are in *From Culture Wars to Common Ground*, a text that Gallagher knows. Our view of equal regard is thick, not thin and flat. It learns from Kant's second version of the categorical imperative, which tells us to treat humanity in both oneself and in others as an end and never as a means alone.[5] Our view of equal regard treats the marital partner with respect in all spheres of life — domestic, religious, and political. But the ethic of equal regard also tells us to work actively for the *good* of the other. It fully realizes that the goods of life are somewhat different for men and women, husbands and wives, fathers and mothers, parents and children. Hence, there will be and must be different roles and tasks between husbands and wives to meet different and evolving needs and goods. This point, and what it means for the proper definition of the equal-regard marriage and family, Gallagher has not fully grasped.

First, a quote from my essay in this volume: "But the idea of neighbor love — and the concept of equal regard between husband and wife that it implies — does not give a complete ethic for families. More is needed." In these words, I am, in effect, agreeing with Gallagher that an ethic of equal regard between husband and wife, as important as it is, is not enough. It must function within a larger cultural and religious narrative that balances the male problematic. The male problematic, as Gallagher and I (and John Miller as well) seem to agree, is the tendency

5. For a discussion of our use of Kant, see Don Browning, Bonnie Miller-McLemore, Pamela Cauture, K. Brynolf Lyon, and Robert Franklin, *From Culture Wars to Common Ground: Religion and the American Family Debate* (Louisville: Westminster/John Knox, 1997), chap. 10.

of males to procreate but often be reluctant to bond with and care for children and wife. This is where the symbols of the Christian faith — the caring fatherhood of God and the love of Christ for the church — have in the past played and can still in the future play such a powerful role. Christian men are asked to identify both with the caring love of God the Father *and* with the love of Christ for the church and to apply this to wife and children. This love is to be permanent and enduring, and it simultaneously *elevates* Christian men in their identification with God and *lowers* them in steadfast servanthood. This twofold movement of elevation and humble servanthood is crucial for understanding how the male problematic is balanced and channeled in Christian symbolism. This symbolism builds on, extends, and makes more enduring natural, but ambiguous, male tendencies to attach to wife and care for children. But this identification with God and Christ does not necessarily imply male headship and does not, as I suggest below, exclude women from such identification as well.

Both Gallagher and Miller seem to miss this symbolism, my elaboration of how it works in the opening essay in this volume, and its detailed development in chapters 4, 5, and 10 in *From Culture Wars to Common Ground*. Furthermore, my colleagues and I fully acknowledge that men have special contributions to make to families. Our position is not a theory of "soft androgyny," as Gallagher suggests. Remember, I fully acknowledged in the opening essay the asymmetrical reproductive strategies of males and females. My colleagues and I know, as did Aquinas, that females carry the infant, that infant dependency puts great pressures on mothers, that this natural condition leads mothers to turn to fathers for help, and, as evolutionary psychology has also argued, that men have ambiguous tendencies to respond to this call and take care of infants who reflect them. These are the natural but unstable energies that go into family formation, energies that the ethic of equal regard builds on and that the symbolism of God the Father and Christ's love for the church extends, stabilizes, and makes enduring.

In chapter 10 of *From Culture Wars to Common Ground* we develop a life-cycle theory of equal regard; in other words, equal regard takes different forms at different stages of life. Clearly, around the conception and birth of a child, men must protect and provide for their wives and children in even more energetic ways. This heightened male mobilization may last for months, possibly for years. Fathers must contribute to the care of children and their mothers. Men in principle must be willing to spend extra energy on behalf of their wives and children indefinitely. During the vulnerabilities of pregnancy and childbirth, mothers may have special connection with and care for their children, but it is also the case that in our society this period may be relatively brief. Soon parenthood, child care, and many other aspects of family life should become once again a matter of equal partnership between husband and wife. Even then, husbands' and wives' duties do not need to be identical. The pattern of equal regard takes many different forms at different points in the life cycle of a marriage, but this does not mean that men must not be active lovers, protectors, providers, and helpers even though the concrete patterns of such actions may change depending on the stage of life.

Families need authority, but this does not require that the male must be the final authority and that the female must be submissive. Husband and wife can create patterns of family authority by interpreting together Bible, tradition, and experience and by dialoguing together in mutuality and equal regard to establish the religious narrative, values, and moral principles that will govern their marriage and parenting. This dialogue is intersubjective because it takes with equal seriousness the interpretive contributions of both husband and wife and requires becoming interior to and sympathetic with each other's thoughts and feelings. This dialogue can gradually include the children as they move toward being competent interpreters themselves. But this developing family dialogue is not just between people who stand outside time and history. If it is a Christian dialogue, it also includes the Christian Scriptures and classics, their ideals and claims, and their capacity to interpret us as we interpret them. And, indeed, in contrast to Gallagher's fear, family authority achieved through dialogue between husband and wife need not talk about every detail of life and should not go on constantly; "equal-regard couples" can and do settle most things. Through dialogue, couples can indeed create a relatively stable family culture and authority.

Gallagher is concerned about overcoming the male problematic. Miller is too. But both forget what we in *From Culture Wars to Common Ground* called the "female problematic" — the tendency of mothers under certain circumstances to bond with the children, exclude the father, and sometimes assert independence and go it alone. Wives and mothers often, due to neglect and poor treatment by husband or lover, have good reason to do this. But sometimes the message of the importance of steadfastness and endurance in marital relationships must be applied as much to wives and mothers as it is to husbands and fathers. This is why we extend — as, in our opinion, the Bible does as well — the balancing factors of Christian symbolism to wives and mothers as well as to husbands and fathers. Wives and mothers should identify with the steadfast love of Christ for the church and apply it to their relations to husband and children. They too are called to sacrificial love, but the goal of such actions is to restore strained or broken family relations to mutuality and equal regard. Mutuality, not self-sacrifice itself, is the ultimate goal. This point is consistent with the gospel; it is also required to protect women from having calls of sacrificial love be transformed into programs of oppression.

Women can be agents of this restoration, this redemption. This, we believe, is the full meaning of Paul's words, "For the unbelieving husband is made holy through his wife" (I Cor. 7:14). This means that the wife can be Christ to the husband just as the husband can mediate the love of Christ to the wife. Enduring love — going the second mile in the effort to restore mutual love — is the vocation of both husband and wife. This is the Christian contribution to overcoming the male and female problematics. This is the distinctive contribution of sacrificial love to the love ethic of equal regard.

I conclude with a warm thanks to Allan Carlson, John Miller, Robert Godfrey, Daniel Cere, and Maggie Gallagher for extending this joint effort to deepen our Christian ethics for marriage and family.

Contributors

David Blankenhorn is founder and president of the Institute for American Values. His publications include *Fatherless America: Confronting Our Most Urgent Social Problem* and *Promises to Keep: Decline and Renewal of Marriage in America* (which he edited with David Popenoe and Jean Bethke Elshtain).

Don Browning is the Alexander Campbell Professor of Ethics and the Social Sciences at the University of Chicago Divinity School. He is also the director of the Project on Religion, Culture, and Family, which has published a twelve-book series.

Allan C. Carlson is the president of the Howard Center for Family, Religion, and Society, an independent operating division of the Rockford Institute, where Dr. Carlson was president from 1986 to 1997. In 1988 he was appointed by President Reagan to the National Commission on Children, and in 1997 he served as General Secretary and lead convenor of The World Congress of Families, held in Prague. His books include *The Family in America: Searching for Social Harmony in the Industrial Age.*

Lisa Sowle Cahill is the J. Donald Monan, S.J., Professor at Boston College, where she has taught theology since 1976. She is a past president of both the Catholic Theological Society of America and the Society of Christian Ethics. Her books include *Sex, Gender, and Christian Ethics* and *Family: A Christian Social Perspective.*

Daniel Mark Cere is the director of the Newman Centre at McGill University, Montreal, Canada. He is also the founder and director of

Institute for the Study of Marriage, Law and Culture. His research interests are in the area of ethics, marriage and family.

Maggie Gallagher is president of the Institute for Marriage and Public Policy in Washington, D.C. and co-author of *The Case for Marriage*. She is also a syndicated columnist.

W. Robert Godfrey is president of Westminster Theological Seminary in Escondido, California. He is also Professor of Church History. An ordained minister in the Christian Reformed Church and a former editor of the *Westminster Theological Journal*, he is a noted author and contributor to numerous publications and has most recently authored *Reformation Sketches: Insights into Luther, Calvin, and the Confessions*.

John W. Miller is Professor of Religious Studies Emeritus at Conrad Grebel College, University of Waterloo. With Professor Paul Hollenbach, he was the co-founder and co-chair of the Society of Biblical Literature. He is the author most recently of *Calling God "Father": Essays on the Bible, Fatherhood, and Culture*.

Bonnie Miller-McLemore is Associate Professor of Pastoral Theology and Counseling at the Divinity School, Vanderbilt University, in Nashville. A co-author of *From Culture Wars to Common Ground: Religion and the American Family Debate*, her other works include *Feminist and Womanist Pastoral Theology: Implications for Care, Faith, and Reflection* (of which she is a co-editor) and *Let the Children Come: Reimaging Childhood from a Christian Perspective*.

Carolyn Osiek is Professor of New Testament at the Catholic Theological Union in Chicago, Illinois. Her works include *Shepherd of Hermas: A Commentary; Families in the New Testament World* (with David Balch); and commentaries on several books of the Bible.

Mary Stewart Van Leeuwen is a social and cross-cultural psychologist who is resident scholar at Eastern University's Center for Christian Women in Leadership. She has had field appointments at York University in Toronto and Calvin College in Michigan. Among her most recent books are *Religion, Feminism, and the Family* (co-edited with Anne Carr), and *My Brother's Keeper: What the Social Sciences Do (and Don't) Tell Us about Masculinity*.

John Witte Jr. is the Jonas Robitscher Professor of Law and Ethics and Director of the Law and Religion Program at Emory Law School. His publications include *From Sacrament to Contract: Marriage, Religion, and Law in the Western Tradition* and *The Essential Rights and Liberties of Religion in America.*